3. APATHETIC
MEDIOCRE EXPRESSION
CONVENTIONAL - IMITATIVE
LACKING SPONTANEITY &
ORIGINALITY

2. CAN'T DO IT
CLOSED THE LIGHT OF
IDEA - LITTLE OR NO
EXPRESSION

1. SELF-CENTERED
THOUGHT TURNS INWARD
NO LISTENING - IDEA-BLOCKED
OUT - TOTAL DARKNESS

Description of chart on Page 226

SPEAK FOR YOURSELF

JESSICA SOMERS DRIVER

SPEAK FOR YOURSELF
essentials of reading aloud and speaking

REVISED EDITION

HARPER & BROTHERS · PUBLISHERS · NEW YORK

Library of Congress catalog card number: 55-11267

Contents

PAGE

Improve Your Speech. It is of Prime Importance to You   1

Part I   THE SCIENCE OF EXPRESSION

Chapter 1   THE STARTING POINT   9

Chapter 2   THE THREE ESSENTIALS   12

Chapter 3   LISTENING   16

Chapter 4   VALUE YOUR ABILITY TO EXPRESS IDEAS   22

Chapter 5   VISUALIZING   31

Chapter 6   SPONTANEITY   38

Chapter 7   RHYTHM   44

Part II   READING ALOUD—An Aid to Better Speaking

Chapter 8   THE FIRST STEP   53

Chapter 9   GOOD CONVERSATIONAL STYLE   61

Chapter 10   CONVERSATIONAL PRONUNCIATION   63

Chapter 11   LAWS OF CONVERSATIONAL READING   67

Chapter 12   NATURAL USE OF THE VOICE   94

Chapter 13   PRESERVE THE BEAUTY OF THE ENGLISH LANGUAGE   105

Chapter 14   THE FINE ART OF READING ALOUD   115

Part III   POISE—Its Relation to Posture and Platform Work

Chapter 15   POISE   147

			PAGE
Chapter 16	POSTURE		153
Chapter 17	ON THE PLATFORM		160

Part IV EXTEMPORANEOUS SPEAKING

Chapter 18	LAWS OF EXTEMPORANEOUS SPEAKING	173
Chapter 19	SHORT TALKS IN OPEN MEETINGS	180
Chapter 20	TO CONDUCT A GROUP MEETING—A CONFERENCE	182
Chapter 21	CONVERSATION	189
Chapter 22	SELLING	197
Chapter 23	INTRODUCTIONS—ANNOUNCEMENTS	204
Chapter 24	LONG TALKS	209

To Commit to Memory	217
Free Expression	225
Key to Transcriptions	235
Index	239

SPEAK FOR YOURSELF

IMPROVE YOUR SPEECH
IT IS OF PRIME IMPORTANCE TO YOU

Try a day of complete silence and see how far you get in your routine contacts!

Those close to you would soon become alarmed, then aggravated, if you tried to communicate with them through some other means than speech. You could not answer your telephone, dictate letters, take part in a conference, sell a product or idea. Before the day was over you would surely gain a deep respect for the part speech plays in your life.

Why, then, don't we make an effort to develop the full potentialities of our speech?

We place ourselves in houses and offices which are as attractive and commodious as possible; we give time and thought to the selection of suitable and becoming clothes; but our speech —that by which we express our thoughts and feelings to others, that by which our education and character are immediately judged—is usually left to chance, largely dependent upon the region and environment of our youth.

Most of us do not placidly accept the methods and equipment of our parents as good enough for us, but we are apt to drift along with their dialects and tone qualities, or with the hesitant and negative habits of speaking formed in childhood, as if these things were as natural and unescapable as the color of our eyes.

We may heartily agree that we express ourselves inadequately and that our speech is not pleasant to the ear. "But," we will add with finality, "it's natural for me to talk this way. Of course, I like to hear people who express themselves well and have good diction, but if I talked that way, I'd sound affected."

Fear of affectation! Here is the reason people are reluctant to attempt any change in their speech. And it is true that certain kinds of training do make one self-conscious and stilted because they exaggerate enunciation and voice mechanics. You say—and rightly—that you prefer crudity to this!

However, when a testing time comes—let us say that you are called upon to appear in public—you become apprehensive. "Just be natural," your friends glibly tell you. But you find, when you start across the platform or stand up to speak, that *you do not know how to be natural.* You are conscious of your hands, your feet, your clothing; you discover you do not know when or how to begin, your thoughts are confused, you are not sure of your voice. An actor wrote, "Naturalness, of all things, is the most difficult to attain," and you agree with him and acknowledge that you need some sort of help if you are ever again to appear before the public.

But you wonder, *"Can I study speech and still be natural?"*

Yes. The right kind of study should show you how to overcome self-consciousness and appear natural even when you are in a trying situation. Many of the suggestions made in this book can be put into immediate use to this end.

You may feel that you will never have to talk in public, but demands are being made upon people these days far beyond their expectations. If one is engaged in any useful work, he is apt to be asked to explain his methods to others, either extemporaneously or with prepared material, so why not be ready for a new experience instead of dodging it?

This book is not only for the professional lecturer, but for the woman who has a home to manage and necessary contacts to make, for the man asking his employer for a raise, or the foreman outlining work for his men. It is not alone for the after-dinner speaker, but for the woman opening a charge account, or the citizen longing to express an opinion in a public meeting, the committee chairman reading a report, or the traveler or hero asked to speak over the radio or appear on television. It is for the poor conversationalist; for the one confused by groups.

Have you ever felt that you had failed to meet a situation, and then, perhaps as you drove home, thought of all the things you could have said but didn't? When it was too late the ideas came spontaneously, without conscious effort on your part, not by means of a slow figuring-out process. You've said to yourself, "Why couldn't I have thought of those things when I needed them?" The laws of extemporaneous speaking will show you how to do just this—bring to mind the things you know at the moment you need them.

Extemporaneous speaking is a science. One can learn it. And it is worth the effort because one is unconsciously influenced by the way people express themselves. We avoid the conversational monopolist, the loud-voiced back-slapper, the hesitant but persistent detail-explainer. But everyone enjoys being around the one whose speech is vivid and to the point.

Reading aloud is also a science based on laws. Contrary to general opinion, words grouped together into sentences for the purpose of giving an idea, take on a certain pattern in pure reading. With an understanding of the laws of reading, you are able to give the full meaning of the words, to read them the way that a good speaker would say them if he were extemporizing.

An executive in a government electronics laboratory attended a course of my lectures. He said some of the leading scientists of the country were at work in that laboratory. They often prepared papers on their discoveries, which were of world-wide interest. These papers were read to a select group, but the reading was so poor that it was impossible to grasp the substance of the thought. Only after the articles were published in current magazines could he get what they contained. He gave these men some of the laws of reading learned in my lectures. They were quick to apply them because they found that these laws enabled them to read ideas instead of mere words.

Many occasions call for reading aloud. In business and in clubs there is often the need for the reading of important information, financial reports, minutes, reading back dictated letters. The politician must understand reading if he would persuade others by means of written speeches. All actors must know how to "read lines." In the religious world it is especially necessary as reading is used to a certain extent in most religious services.

Reading aloud is also used almost exclusively in presenting radio programs. Haven't you turned on your radio and known instantly that the one speaking was inexperienced? You listen a moment and find that it is an author being interviewed, or a baseball player endorsing a product, or an eminent business-man giving valuable data. The script he reads has been prepared by skilled writers from his own words, and yet he reads it with such false emphasis, stilted pronunciation and faulty timing that its force is lost, sometimes even to the point of absurdity.

On the other hand, if the person is experienced he sounds as if he were talking to you in your own home. Sincerity gives his words dignity and power, and his voice beauty, warmth and appeal.

Part II of this book is devoted to laws of reading which will show you how to bring the conviction of conversation into what you read.

It has been proved too often that the study of speech techniques alone does not ensure free expression. A Foreign Minister who addressed a select group of citizens, eager to receive his message, put them to sleep by reading a long scholarly report. He was a highly educated man, having studied and taught in many countries; he was well qualified to present his subject for he had been instrumental in forming crucial treaties of world-wide concern; but he did not know how to bring these ideas to his listeners in a forceful way. He did not understand what I call the *science of expression*.

This science slipped into my experience almost without my knowing it. Some time after I had stopped my formal education, I studied with Emma Dunn, an excellent actress and teacher. She taught me the fine art of reading aloud, how to read with the conviction of speaking, and awakened me to the great part inspiration plays in expression. Then when I began to teach adult classes, I gave them that which had been helpful to me and constantly reached out for better ways to meet each student's need. Through many years of analyzing good and poor expression, through my own experience before the public, and especially through working with people to help them express themselves more freely, certain basic truths became clear to me. As I wrote them down, I discovered that these truths dovetailed into a consistent whole. Perhaps because I had majored in mathematics, I began to suspect that expression was a science, based on invariable principles and rules.

I knew that if it were a science, it would appear in the accomplishments of outstanding people. I observed and questioned prominent businessmen, artists, musicians, and found that while most of them would attribute their success to entirely different causes, *they had complied with these laws* whenever they had expressed themselves freely.

I noticed that free expression is a fundamental aim in all education. The engineer studies mathematics, engineering design, strength of materials, that he may express ideas—for instance, span a river with a bridge, or design the structure of a skyscraper. The artist, writer, musician, architect, takes innumerable subjects in schools for the sole purpose of being able to express himself freely in his own particular mode. As a result of over a quarter of a century's study, I come to this conclusion: Free expression is not something which can be attained only through a trial and failure procedure. It is not a mysterious gift bestowed at birth, or by some quirk of fate, on a special few.

Free expression is a science. It can be learned.

For many years now, I have based my courses on this science. Its laws give the students a firm foundation from which to work. Inhibitions of long standing have been dropped and efficiency and freedom gained. Timid persons, when they have learned these basic principles, have accepted and done well in positions which previously they would have turned down. Others have received promotions as they have learned to express themselves more freely. Knowledge of free expression has also been a stimulus to originality and good performance in the arts, and gives the key to genuine art appreciation. A president of a national organization wrote, "The principles you teach . . . have proved very helpful in the speaking requirements of my business . . . but they are really the opening of a door to interest and understanding of almost all of the arts. . . ." The New York district manager of another national firm said that this approach had given him a freedom almost like "a new, an additional gear."

It is therefore with conviction that I present the laws of expression. While they may appear simple, they are basic, and important to you. It is these laws which have brought freedom to the students.

Now to define terms as they are used in this book. Exactly what is meant by expression?

PART I

THE SCIENCE OF EXPRESSION

Chapter *1*

THE STARTING POINT

Expression is the act of bringing an *idea* into view, of giving it a tangible form. For instance, the idea of giving farmers a place to display their products speedily, without having to go through the hands of a middleman, found expression in the building of a farmers' market. The idea of wanting a newcomer to meet your friends leads to the giving of a party. Frequently an appreciation of the idea of beauty and order seen in nature causes one to garden, redecorate his home, or compose a symphony. All expression, be it business, art, social intercourse or science, comes into existence because of an idea—an idea entertained until it becomes so clear that the one seeing it is impelled to bring it out in some definite form.

Naturally, then, *idea* is the starting point in the analysis of expression.

But *idea* is a word that varies widely in connotation. Hegel defined it as "the absolute truth of which all phenomenal existence is the expression; the Idea, the Absolute." Descartes and Locke held it as "the immediate object of thought or mental perception." Plato called it "an eternally existing pattern of any class of things, of which the individual things are imperfect copies, and from which they derive their existence."

Idea is used here in an absolute sense as synonymous with truth, fact, inner reality, ideal, not in the relative sense of an opinion or impression.

There are two characteristics of an idea which have a direct bearing on expression.

   I. *An idea is impersonal.*

   II. *An idea includes all that is necessary for its expression.*

9

The first point, that an idea is impersonal:

Never is it *my* idea, but an idea which I see—available to anyone, belonging to no one. Since it is truth, it is discovered, not created by someone.

The fact that the same invention often comes into the patent office almost simultaneously from different parts of the world indicates this impersonal character of an idea. The first models of television were sent in at the same time by two men working independently. Their models were practically identical.

The second point, an idea includes all that is necessary for its expression:

See an idea clearly, eliminating any sense of inadequacy or personal responsibility, and you may rest assured that you can show it forth in some form. The necessary technique for its expression, the right word or phrase, is included in the idea; so also is the dynamic impetus which urges you into action.

A college student's excuse, "I know but I can't express it," was answered by one of his professors, "You don't know well enough." Experience had taught this professor that an idea can always be expressed if it is understood.

A prehistoric man lighted his way at night with a burning branch. That action was not personal, but a crude and practical expression of the idea of illumination. Modern science, with a clearer concept of this idea, now brings it out by building elaborate networks of wiring to connect distant points with the source of electrical power. As a result we get light by the mere closing of a switch. Both the burning branch and the electric system are expressions of the same idea, produced in a form adapted to the age in which the expression appears.

The expression is as close to perfection as one's concept is to the idea. Concept is used here in its relative sense, as a personal view of an idea. The concept may change; the idea never.

How well Beethoven proved the expressive power within ideas. He wrote: "I can almost grasp them with my hands in the open air, in the woods, while walking, in the stillness of the night, early in the morning, called up by moods which the poet translates into words, I into musical tones. They ring and roar and swirl about me until I write them down in notes." (*Beethoven—The Man and the Artist as Revealed in His Own Words*, by Kerst and Krehbiel.)

What quality of thought enabled him to grasp ideas in this way? Is it something we can acquire? It is self-evident that the first need of expression is an idea. How do we get ideas?

Chapter 2

THE THREE ESSENTIALS

There are three steps which one takes when he expresses an idea—listening, valuing, expressing.

I. *Listening*

The word *listening* is used literally and figuratively. Whenever a listening attitude is reached, ideas come—not from sound alone, but often as a spontaneous influx of thoughts, sometimes called *inspiration*.

This word *inspiration* is not used here as a special dispensation to the elect, or as an emotional exhilaration, but is used to define a process as natural and universal as breathing. In fact, the word is often used in connection with breathing to denote the indrawing of breath—*inspiration*—in contrast to *expiration* —breathing out. But *inspiration* also means the awakening to ideas; *expression,* the giving out of these ideas. You need inspiration for expression just as you do for breathing.

When Charles Laughton read the "Gettysburg Address" he listened with appreciation as he spoke, and those who heard him were newly impressed by the depth and timeliness of Lincoln's words. It is this listening attitude which brings inspiration into his nightly performances and invariably draws enthusiastic audiences.

Since listening is essential to inspired expression, the first question is, "How can I learn to listen?"

Quietness is the first requirement. If you tell a group to listen, the first thing they do is to quiet down. But mere physical stillness is not enough. You may preserve a quiet exterior while inwardly you feel as if an egg beater has stirred you up. There must be mental calmness as well. Balance this with alertness, interest, focus.

To test your ability to listen, try it now for several moments. Listen with the whole of you, from the top of your head to the tips of your toes. Really take time to do it.................
. . . .

Where was your thought turned as you listened? You will find it was focused away from self—outward.

Listening stops "self" consciousness.

It is as easy as that. When thought is turned completely away from self in listening, you cannot be self-conscious.

When you listened just now did you feel a peaceful quiet sense replace the tension which comes from the hurried tempo of present-day living? There is no strain in true listening, only a positive expectant readiness. In this mood you become aware of the ideas you need for the job at hand.

The next step:

II. *Value the idea*

When you value an idea, you stay with it until you understand it. Valuing also leads you to seek the technique for your particular need. Some persons think that a passing thrill is enough to carry them on to good performance; they often say they work inspirationally and do not need to study technique. Usually they have only glimpsed the idea and are too superficial, or think it too much trouble, to follow through with it. *But an idea, valued, will not let you be idle.* You are pushed into doing something about it. While the common definition of genius as "the capacity for taking infinite pains" is far from true—since dull drudgery never made a genius—still, nothing is too much work for the one inspired with an idea. An inspired person reaches results much more surely and quickly than the one who works mechanically on technique alone, for the idea is constantly stimulating him.

Whether or not an idea is suitable to your use at present shows up in this valuing step. But be slow to discard an idea as untimely. It usually comes because you are ready for it.

A man in a corporation had attended one class of our Basic Course in expression. In a business meeting a vital issue of his company had been presented and discussed, and because no solution could be reached the meeting was finally adjourned. In thinking it over later an idea came to him. Ordinarily he would have let it drop with the habitual feeling that he would never think of anything worth while. This time, because of what he had learned in the class, he valued the idea, stayed with it and clarified it to himself, knew it was impersonal, and presented it in this way at the adjourned meeting. To his surprise it was unanimously accepted.

A middle-aged woman who was so shy that she would scarcely speak even in a small group was given the educational truth that an idea includes all that is necessary for its expression. She valued this thought, and as a result, when asked to address some people on a subject that she understood thoroughly, she consented—though with misgivings. Upon being introduced, she looked out at the people and, as she had expected, her mind became a blank. Standing there, she thought, "Why did I ever do this, I never can talk, and now look at the predicament that I'm in! I'll certainly never try this again. But what shall I do now? Oh, I was told to think only of the idea." The subject she loved came into her thought. Reassured, she started to talk, giving an explanation that was so comprehensive that it amazed the friends who knew of her reticence. After that one experience, she was unafraid to talk at any time, disproving the old-fashioned theory that educational processes need to be lengthy, especially with adults.

In reading, the valuing step causes you to think of every word as you say it. This does not mean that every word is emphasized. Far from it! Only new-idea words are given value, and the many unimportant ones, or those which give nothing new, are put in the background. If you are undistracted, this valuing can take place very quickly—as quickly as words are put together in talking.

A talented composer whose songs usually came to him in the night would get up, even in the middle of winter, light a fire, and work out the composition. Without this high esteem for inspiration he would have lost many beautiful songs. Getting the inspiration of the theme was only the first step. The valuing of it made him follow through until the song was written.

An idea, valued, takes on form and color in thought. You become filled with it. To keep from expressing it would be like trying to stop childbirth. The idea has to appear.

Then you have the next step:

III. *Express the idea*

This expression is easy if the other two steps have been taken. It happens almost in spite of you. However, you must let it come when you feel the urge. Do not hold back because you are afraid to try, or simply because you don't feel inclined to express yourself right now, or perhaps because you think that at another time you will be better prepared. You grow dull to the message if you do not respond to it. Appreciate the idea sufficiently and you will have the technique you need for this particular time—the idea includes it. This lets you say your say in the way that is best for you with your special background— a way that will be original and colorful.

Brief as this theory is, it is far-reaching and practical.

Chapter *3*

LISTENING

A listening attitude is indispensable to good expression. Anything which will help you define the listening attitude to yourself and embody it in your thinking, will increase your poise, your perception, and your expressive ability. This chapter is to help you clarify the idea of listening.

The one who listens is in a state of positive expectancy—like an open hand stretched out to receive something. He is wide-awake and undistracted, his full attention on the thing of the moment, whether it be the word he is reading or the thought he is about to express. "Eye on the ball" is the listener's motto. Still he is unstrained. Thought should be focused outward in listening with as little effort as the sun's rays are focused through a magnifying glass—and the results are as potent.

Many years ago I saw a photograph of a tournament tennis player just before he hit the ball. Everything about the man seemed to be focused on that ball. His identification with what he was doing was so complete that the picture made a lasting impression on me—the wonderful quietness and poise balanced with attention and intention. You instinctively knew that this player had no thought of himself, he was wholly idea-conscious.

What a contrast to the lukewarm way people usually go at things, only a small portion of their thought on the idea they express, the rest on themselves or on those around, or on nothing and everything—just aimlessly wandering.

Then there are many who can listen well for a few moments; but they soon digress—like the Bandar-log, the monkeys in Kipling's *Jungle Book,* always boasting of the great things they were going to do, never accomplishing anything because they

Business Reply Mail No postage stamp necessary if mailed in the United States

Postage will be paid by

LIFE
Time & Life Building
Chicago, Illinois 60611

For colorful coverage of what's happening today. From Washington to Moscow, from fashion fronts to behind sports scenes.

25 WEEKS OF LIFE FOR $2.95

LESS THAN 12¢ A WEEK. WE'LL BILL YOU LATER. NEW SUBSCRIBERS ONLY. GOOD ONLY IN U.S.

name _____

address _____ apt. no. _____

city _____ state _____ zip _____

Also send me 26 weeks of S.I. for $3.97 ☐   Only send me 26 weeks of S.I. for $3.97 ☐

L 8685

were sidetracked so easily. Notice how the real artists have learned to stay with what they are doing, constantly listening, constantly inspired.

Thought needs to be free in order to listen. For example. suppose you were commissioned to write an article on an irreplaceable piece of old ivory, exquisitely carved. The ivory is brought to you to examine. You would not reach for it carelessly, with your hands full of papers. No, you would put everything aside, lest you might drop it. You give it your full attention. This attitude lets you identify yourself with it. The treasure can then seem to speak to you, you become inspired with its beauty and significance. Now you are ready to write about it. You could equally well tell about it, draw it, paint it, appraise it, because you have given yourself a chance to get at the essence of the thing: you have listened to it.

Yet how many times you reach for ideas and fail to get them because your thought is cluttered with preconceived notions, the small details of living, negative thinking, reasoning. The last may startle you, but the fact is that as you start to reason, there is a running to and fro of the thought which stops the spontaneous grasping of truth. Reasoning may come later, not during the taking in of ideas.

This point was aptly put by Robert Henri, that great teacher of painters, in *The Art Spirit,* when he said that intellectuality (a close associate of reason) stops our listening to an idea and expressing while under its spell. "The song (the idea) fills us with surprise. We marvel at it. We would continue to hear it. But few are capable of holding themselves in a state of listening to their own song. Intellectuality steps in, and as the song within us is of the utmost sensitiveness, it retires in the presence of the cold, material intellect." But he goes on to say that "we live in the memory of these songs which in moments of intellectual inadvertence have been possible to us. They are the pinnacles of our experience and it is the desire to express . . .

this song within which motivates the masters of all art." Most of the great contributions to the world have come in these "moments of intellectual inadvertence."

The ideas needed for creative and constructive work are discovered by the listener.

A noted airplane designer, Igor Sikorsky, when addressing the American Society of Mechanical Engineers, said, "Intuition appears to be some ability which permits an inventor, in a way not yet explained and possibly inexplainable, to 'tune in' like a radio and to learn somehow facts or laws that are not yet known, or imagine and create a mechanism or part in correct accord with natural laws not yet discovered at the time of the invention."

It is not schooling which gives a man intuition. It is listening, the open door through which ideas enter.

Dr. Carver, distinguished Negro scientist and wizard in chemical discoveries, realized this. He said that he got up at four o'clock every morning and went out into the woods and listened to what nature had to teach him. The results of this listening—innumerable uses for the peanut and sweet potato, as well as for many other wasted materials—are general knowledge.

Beardsley Ruml, author of the famous "pay as you go" income-tax plan, said that the most important part of his day was the time when he sat alone and did nothing. At this time, he said, various solutions of problems came to him. He called it "a state of dispersed attention." Just sitting and indulging in reverie was not what he did. Judging from the many practical financial and governmental plans he evolved in these periods, he really listened until he got the ideas he needed.

Daydreaming, which masquerades as listening, is an enemy of achievement. The impetus of an idea pushes you into action; you are uncomfortable until you respond to it in some way. Daydreaming brings a certain satisfaction which dulls this impetus. Ideas which are dreamed about are seldom expressed; they are played with—thinking of what the idea might do for you, of what others would say about it, or about you. Young persons are inclined to indulge in this reverie and some never overcome the habit. Unfruitful lives result—lives spent in talking and thinking *about* ideas instead of lives activated by ideas.

This point was given to a group in one of our in-training courses. One who did selling over the telephone came to the next class with this experience: She said that she had been talking to a woman about a $500 order. The woman finally remarked, "I guess I'll daydream about it for a while." The sales person promptly answered, "I've just been taking a course that points out that daydreaming is destructive. When you daydream about a thing you seldom go any further." The client thought a moment, then said, "I believe you're right. Send the contract around. I'll sign it now."

The right sense of imagination should not be confused with daydreaming. Daydreaming is personal musing about an idea. Imagination is the unfolding of ideas in thought. It causes you to do something about them—make a speech, iron out kinks in a business, study the technique of some line of endeavor. It is a necessary part of visualizing.

Listening is the key to learning.

We are educated only by those ideas which reach us. Opportunities for enlightenment such as reading, travel, schooling, leave us untouched unless thought is open and ready to receive. A walk in the country may remain only a walk, an exercise of the legs. But with listening we may go through what we see on the surface to the underlying ideas, we may "hear life murmur and see it glisten."

When you learn to listen you widen your range of interest and your fund of knowledge grows hourly. You are continually being educated. One of the most cultured men I ever knew had not gone beyond high school, but he was a keen listener. When he heard something new he would follow it up in his atlas, dictionary, encyclopedia, until he had informed himself thoroughly. Throughout a long lifetime he was constantly educating himself.

Listening is discriminating.

Often it is asked if this opening of thought might not lead to an acceptance of the spurious as well as the good. An example was cited of an English-educated German girl, who, while in London, clearly saw the errors of the Nazi regime, but upon returning to her own country, for a time wholeheartedly took in the Nazi ideology. The fact is that listening is not just openness. Because it is reaching out for ideas, for truths, it spontaneously rejects the counterfeit without effort. This German girl did not listen; she accepted what was told her. Listening would have caused her to penetrate the fallacies and discover the facts.

True listening overcomes self-consciousness.

Nothing leaves you so delightfully forgetful of self as listening.

An eminent businessman in a large city was made head of the community chest drive for the state, and had to talk on the radio and television, and address groups of workers in many localities. He said: "I have no sense of being inferior to any man on earth. But in spite of my self-confidence, when a group is quietly expecting me to speak, I get nervous." He was told that listening is a means of overcoming self-consciousness, that in listening, thought must necessarily be turned away from self. Instead of arguing about the point, he immediately put it into practice, as good businessmen have a way of doing. His difficulty in talking ceased from that time. He listened carefully to the other speakers, to his introducer, and refused to let his thought turn inward. Rescued from self-conscious-ness, he wrote that what he had learned about listening was "just exactly the right dose of stimulus to transform a weak, frightened chairman into one sufficiently self-confident to get over the speech-making hurdles."

The effects of listening are apparent, not only in the voice and phrasing of the inspired reader, always listening for the ideas back of what he reads, but also in the tournament tennis player moving around the court under its direction. It is called "anticipation" in tennis, but it comes only to the listener who understands tennis and keeps his eye on the ball. The astute businessman gets at the essence of a situation and makes wise judgments because he listens until he comprehends the idea behind the transaction, and lets the idea guide him. In the same way, the words of the speaker come naturally as soon as he turns his thought away from self and listens.

Listening cannot be bought. No one else can make you listen. No one can do it for you—it is not vicarious. Moreover, when you already "know all the answers" you do not listen. You may be awakened to the value of listening and the way may be pointed out for you, but you must open your own door to in-tuition and inspiration by learning to quiet self and listen.

Chapter *4*

VALUE YOUR ABILITY
TO EXPRESS IDEAS

When you think of an idea, if you feel it has worth, you "follow through" with it, stay with it mentally until it is clear to you. This second step of expression I call "valuing the idea." It is that something which happens between the time you see an idea and move into its expression. Sometimes it causes you to spend years in technical study, at other times you may act almost immediately, where controlled skill is not required, but this valuing always occurs before you have expression.

There is also the need of valuing your own ability. Note that successful people usually have confidence in themselves, or, better still, forget themselves completely because of their absorbing interest in what they are doing. Professor Todd of Amherst wrote in this connection, ". . . in my memory of the college men who have made a signal success in the world, I cannot find one who did not display even in college, a certain confidence in his own soul and being, that made him superior to the superficial opinion of the mass. That confidence, I believe, is a real essential."

Egotism is as detrimental to free expression as self-depreciation but it is not as prevalent. Self-depreciation has posed as a virtue called modesty, so it has been readily accepted as a part of one's normal make-up, whereas few have wanted to claim egotism. Even though in recent years the inferiority complex has been exposed as undesirable, many still accept it with the mistaken feeling that it is unescapable.

A club woman read a report for another who was too shy

personalizes and limits the scope of your work. Also pointing out flaws or apologizing for them brings them into prominence. Look at mistakes only long enough to correct them. A wise newspaperman said, "Support the good you do; leave all the defeats behind."

The value placed on your work or words is only as high as you place it on yourself. This may sound strange, but the fact remains that the message and the messenger are placed on the same level. A high sense of your own worth will increase your usefulness.

Ethel Merman shows this respect for herself and her work. When she was asked if she were nervous on her opening nights on Broadway, she said, "I figured it out a long time ago. I know what I'm going to do—the audience doesn't. Let them be nervous! Besides, if the audience could do it any better, they'd be where I am and I'd be sitting out front." She has been described as a lady without qualms. To be "without qualms," without distrust of your ability, you have to know yourself, like yourself, and be yourself.

In one of Jesus' parables, given in Matthew 25, there is a graphic example of the inactivity which results from failure to value one's ability. A man went away on a trip and left his goods in charge of his servants. *"Unto one he gave five talents, to another two, and to another one; to every man according to his several ability."* The first two valued what they had received, and by putting it to use, doubled it. *"But he that had received one went and digged in the earth, and hid his lord's money."* Either he did not value the one talent or else he doubted his ability to use it to advantage. In any event, he covered it up, as we so often do with our talents. When the master returned, he commended the two who by good investment had increased what they received. He said they would be able to do even greater things as a result of their experience.

But he who had been given the one talent started justifying

himself. *"Lord, I knew thee that thou art an hard man, reaping where thou hast not sown, and gathering where thou hast not strewed and I was afraid, and went and hid thy talent in the earth: lo, there thou hast that is thine."* The master harshly rebuked the servant's foolish caution and inactivity. The one unused talent was taken from him and given to the one with the ten talents and the slothful servant was told *"unto everyone that hath* (we might add, in the light of the whole parable, everyone that hath initiative and a right value of his ability) *shall be given, and he shall have abundance: but from him that hath not shall be taken away even that which he hath."*

"Comparisons are odorous," said Shakespeare. When you compare yourself with another, either you feel inferior, "Oh, what's the use; I never could speak as well as he does"; or superior, "Watch me!" Both of these interfere with your naturalness. You may learn from another's work, but remember that what is right for one person may not be right for you. Your backgrounds are different. You stand at different points of observation so you get different views. Value what you yourself know, without comparison.

When you know within yourself that you have done a thing well, you have a kindly feeling toward the world. But when you repress the ideas which come to you, and do not express them, they rankle within you causing a fruitless unsatisfied feeling. This almost always takes outward form in criticism of those who are expressive—probably in the effort to ease the unpleasant sense of your own shortcomings.

A young writer won overnight popularity and was repeatedly invited to speak in the local clubs. Being used to country life, she felt uneasy when she was brought into an atmosphere where clothes and etiquette played an important role. She took refuge in an attitude of exaggerated crudity and railed against the people who she thought caused her discomfort. But in her writing there was no such attitude. There she was fully with the idea and she warmly, graciously welcomed the readers to share her outdoor experiences. There was never any taint of the belligerent girl who thought she loved animals and disliked people. She could have included this same freedom in her speaking assignments if she had valued her ability to speak as she did her ability to write. The same technique works for both modes of expression.

It is usually our own sense of inadequacy, not the actual lack of ability, which curtails our freedom.

In studying the fundamentals of expression, I have found *Roget's Thesaurus* of inestimable value. It not only offers synonyms of the fundamental word being studied, showing the qualities which are associated with it, but it also shows in the antonyms the temperamental tendencies which are detrimental to this particular fundamental and need to be avoided.

Of course, you have to select that which will be helpful for your expression. For instance, if you were working on the word *positive,* you would find under that word, *certainty, sure, well-founded, clear, decisive*—fine qualities to include in your way of stating things. But you would also find the extremes of *positive—dogmatic, opinionated, dictatorial*—most undesirable traits to have.

There is no such thing as a real synonym, for every word has a shade of distinction in its meaning. Still Roget shows the kind of company a word keeps and will often give you facets of its meaning which are not discovered in a definition. It is advisable to look over all the parts of speech under the word you are studying, because it is not an exact synonym you are seeking but a richer sense of its qualities with regard to expression.

Here are a few contrasting words taken from synonyms and antonyms of the word *value.* They appealed to me. Others might appeal to you. The synonyms show the qualities which will help you to value an idea and your ability to express it, while the antonyms show habits and attitudes which retard your expression.

VALUE

appreciate	depreciate
mark with a white stone	take no notice of
prize, uphold, esteem	not be able to say much for
estimate	swallow whole
set a price on	mark down
write in letters of gold	discredit
be important	second fiddle
be somebody	feel like two cents
deserve regard	mediocre
<u>color value</u>	colorless, dull (Do you know
<u>bright, fresh, gay</u>	any voices like these?)

Use a "take it or leave it" tone of impersonal conviction, just as you would say "two and two are four." When you try to get approval you use an ingratiating tone, quite different from that used when you are stating a fact or are engrossed in your subject and only desirous of sharing it with others. Then you are neither apologetic nor aggressive.

Maintain this even keel even in the face of praise. Bulwer Lytton said, "There is no weapon that slays its victim so surely (if well aimed) as praise." You may be the victim of praise. A man who was in the public eye was asked if he had been told that he had a beautiful voice. He reluctantly admitted that he had. The question was asked because his tone showed that he was listening to the sound of his voice. But one who knew how to take praise impersonally said, when complimented on his performance, "I enjoyed it too." And why not? Ideas are impersonal. He didn't feel that the credit belonged to him.

At the beginning of their training, Jesus gave his disciples this lesson in right valuation. He told them, "Ye are the salt of the earth. . . . Ye are the light of the world. A city that is set on an hill cannot be hid. Neither do men light a candle, and put it under a bushel, but on a candlestick; and it giveth light unto all that are in the house. Let your light so shine before men . . ." (Matt. 5:13-16). He knew that if they saw their own importance, they would make the world value more highly what they said and did. They could not be useful in spreading his doctrine unless they had this appreciation of themselves and were impressed with the importance of what they taught. He said in substance: You are a daily need to the world, its light. Don't go around with a shrinking attitude. Put that light on a candlestick. After all, you know, it isn't your person which gives the light. It is the candle flame, the ideas you offer. Let them be seen!

Have you ever quietly, sincerely, told yourself that you are the light of the world? Try doing it. You will not feel proud but purposeful and poised—gracious toward all who are around you.

Hide not your talents; they for use were made.
What is a sun-dial in the shade?—FRANKLIN

What you need is to free yourself from your own preconceived ideas about yourself. . . .
Work always as if you were a master, expect from yourself a masterpiece. . . .
A small boy can be a master. I have met masters now and again, some in studios, others anywhere, working on a railroad, running a boat, playing a game, selling things. . . .
Masters of such as they had. They are wonderful people to meet. Have you never felt yourself "in the presence" when with a carpenter, or a gardener? When they are the right kind they do not say, "I am only a carpenter or a gardener, therefore not much can be expected from me." They say or they seem to say, "I am a Carpenter"; "I am a

Gardener!" These are masters, what more could anyone be?

Masters are people who use what they have.—HENRI

A school of psychology was developed at Columbia University by the late Prescott Lecky called the "theory of self-consistency." This psychological theory, which resulted from seven years of study and research by Prof. Lecky, rejected the dogma that man is a machine and held that man must be thought of as a unit in himself, a system that operates as a whole. . . . The nucleus of the system around which the rest of the system revolves is the *individual's conception of himself.*

Not the humility that thinks disparagingly of self, but the better humility that forgets self altogether.

                                        —HENRY DRUMMOND

As a man thinketh in his heart, so is he.   BIBLE

Chapter 5
VISUALIZING

More important to success than any amount of technique is the power to visualize. It is visualizing that enables the reader to give you the "feel" of his text, not merely a clear photographic reproduction of it. His reading brings you actual experience. The salesman who knows how to visualize is the one who presents his product or idea so that you know just what it is and what it will do for you. You buy from this salesman. The speaker who visualizes, expressing himself so vividly that the listener, without effort, is able to follow and enjoy each thing that is related, is in constant demand. Some have this gift from birth, but it can be learned.

What do we mean by the term *visualizing?* In this work we mean the ability to picture mentally something not actually present to the senses and then to express it, give it a concrete form.

As mentioned previously, the three steps of expression are listening, valuing and expressing. When you listen to an idea and value it, you stay with it until you reach its essence and understand it. You visualize it to yourself. Then, because an idea is dynamic it sets you in motion—you express it, you actualize it almost without conscious effort. You visualize it to others.

Some will look at an idea intellectually, perhaps analyze it and classify it, but always keep it at arm's length. As a result their expression is conventional and uninspired. Others will approach an idea with apathy, satisfied merely to scratch the surface. A warm response to the idea, an appreciation of it, must precede words that are to stir and impress the imagination of the listener.

A woman who came to California with no experience in selling but with the need to make a living, went into real estate. As a result of taking one of our courses, her ability to visualize was sharpened and amplified. When she had a piece of property to advertise she would never offer mere statistics such as, "A six room house with three bedrooms and two baths." Instead she would go to the location by herself and quietly listen for inspiration as to what the property had to offer. Her ads would be more likely to read, "A haven of peace away from the hurly-burly, yet only a few minutes from the village. A small home, but with a large living room highlighted by an old brick fireplace and homey book shelves. Three roomy bedrooms. Sunny yellow kitchen. All yours for $17,500, and there's wonderful financing."

Her success was so immediate that real estate brokers in the neighboring towns were forced to change their prosaic advertising methods to more colorful ones.

Much emphasis has been placed on the study of technique, and it is desirable, but unless a student understands the science of expression and the art of visualizing which expression demands, he does not use his technique to advantage. I watched Lotte Lehmann teaching German lieder to a master class of young and promising singers. In many cases she was able to give them the feel of the song through her criticisms, by presenting searching questions to make them think, or by half whispering, half singing the words so they would get the mood. At other times she would deplore, "You do what I tell you to do, but that is not it. You are just imitating me. You must go deeper. See what I see. Feel what I feel." Her great contribution to them was teaching them to visualize as they sang—an absolute essential for a great singer.

Visualizing can also move people to action. In one of my classes the assignment was to give an announcement that would arouse interest. One student read a notice of a Mexican restaurant at Padua Hills, California, that presented a play following the dinner. The notice was received with polite stillness by the class. Then someone spoke up and said she had been there recently and saw a sunset that rivaled the desert for color. She said the place was set in the semidesert foothills of the Sierras commanding a wide expanse of view across the valley. Then she told of the waiters and waitresses, all young Mexicans in costume, playing soft rhythmic Mexican music, singing and dancing their native dances during the dinner hour for the guests' entertainment. After dinner she said that the guests wandered out under the olive trees to the shops which displayed Mexican and other art objects. Then came the rollicking play depicting life in Mexico, the audience at times even being part of the play.

Immediately following this spontaneous recital, several of the out-of-town students wanted to know how to get there and all the details about the place. The first person gave the vital statistics but met with no response; the second, by visualizing, moved the listeners to action.

Some of the synonyms and antonyms for visualizing given in *Roget's Thesaurus* are:

VISUALIZE

realize	not understand
imaginative	visionless
inspiration	lack of discernment
alive to	unmoved
in focus	distorted
tip toe of expectation	unresponsive
look full in the face	mist before the eyes
exteriority	interiority
objectify	keep within
actualize	withhold
envisage	imprison
originality	imitation
accurate	inexact
pregnant with meaning	dead letter

When a class studies visualizing I often assign the words "dead letter" also. A dead letter is one which never reaches its destination, and speech without visualization never reaches the listener's comprehension. In fact, empty words, words with no thought in them, are worse than nothing. A silence is strong, but, as the Bible says, "the letter killeth."

I cannot overemphasize how many persons are ineffectual because they are unaware that words alone do not convey an idea. Words must be vital to you before you can visualize with them. Look them up if you do not know their exact meaning. If they have lost their significance through overuse bring them to life with synonyms and antonyms.

The reader who responds to the words with thought and voice until the reading seems actual experience, moves listeners to feel and see what is described.

An an example, here is the way you might work with the 40th Psalm.

> I waited patiently for the Lord; and he inclined unto me, and heard my cry. He brought me up also out of an horrible pit, out of the miry clay, and set my feet upon a rock, and established my goings.

Waited patiently is translated from the original Hebrew expression which means *bound together* (Strong's *Bible Diction-ary**). In Roget, *patiently* is classed with *perseveringly, constantly, undeviatingly, in sickness and in health,* not *irresolutely, half-heartedly, hesitantly* (antonyms of *patiently*). After looking these words over, thoughtfully reread the verses:

> *I waited patiently for the Lord* [I bound myself together with the Lord, constantly, in sickness and in health] *and he inclined unto me and heard my cry. He brought me up also out of an horrible pit* [trap, deception, source of danger, sunken rocks, quicksand, whirlpool, latency—

---

* Found at the end of Strong's *Exhaustive Concordance of the Bible.*

ROGET. He brought me up out of all these things], *out of the miry clay* [that which sticks to my feet, sucks them in, makes progress hard], *and set my feet upon a rock* [according to Roget rock is grouped with stability, safety, not changeableness, danger, chance], *and established* [fixed, made sure, settled], *my goings* [according to the original Hebrew, the word translated *goings* could also mean *prosperity.*—Strong's *Bible Dictionary*].

A deeper understanding of words in this passage cannot fail to open out the meaning for you. Insist that words pay you dividends. Sound their depths. This will increase your apprehension in silent reading and find reflection in your tone and emphasis when reading aloud.

A man in one of my classes said that visualizing had helped him in studying. When I asked him why this was, he said, "You know how quickly and vividly anyone visualizes an accident. I do the same thing when I study. I visualize clear pictures from the words I read and as a result the substance of the text stays with me."

One who came to me for help in public reading was an accomplished dancer. His reading vastly improved when I told him, "Visualize! Make your reading live as much as if you were dancing it. Give us the feel of it. We look at you doing an Indian dance and we think only of an Indian dancing, not of you. We must be able to hear you read and think only of the meaning. Appreciate the meaning deeply yourself. Stay behind every word and see the idea it symbolizes as you say it, instead of hitting the word from the outside."

If you will take your freest activity—whether it may be managing a household or a business, playing golf or gardening—and notice the authoritative way in which you perform, you will have a model to use on all occasions. Robert Henri said, "Like to do your work as much as a dog likes to gnaw a bone and go at it with equal interest and exclusion of everything else."

The keen relish with which a dog tackles a bone and the way he focuses his attention on it, only looking away from it to be sure no one disturbs him, is the way we should go at ideas which we want to visualize.

Many teachers have had their interest in their subject worn thin through repetition. Their fire burns out, they lose their zest and fall into a routine way of explaining their material. No one can possibly grasp the substance of what is said in this thoughtless way. Ministers, lecturers, salesmen, in fact anyone who has to repeat his subject matter, may fall into the same difficulty as teachers.*

Can this large group of people make their speaking more alive and interesting, both to themselves and to their listeners? Yes, visualizing will do it. While they may have to repeat the subject matter, the idea is not the same because each group is different, each day presents a variety of happenings in the world and in their own experience. As they learn to listen for the best way to give their subject to this specific group at this particular moment, their presentation will always be fresh.

Certain habits of thinking retard visualizing.

The apathetic person will not visualize, for it requires that he be alive to what he is doing. He only "sees through a glass darkly." The conservative one will do it only to a limited degree because, if he allows himself to visualize well, it is almost certain to carry him into original ways of expressing himself. He would rather be mediocre than different. The egotist will not do it, for it requires him to forget himself and to be devoted to the ideas he is giving out. The flighty one will not hold himself to what he is doing. Because he lets thought wander he cannot visualize well.

None can be free from dispositional traits at all times. The

* The chapter, "To Commit to Memory," p. 217 will explain how to retain a conversational quality in lectures which must be committed to memory and given verbatim.

fact, however, that the actor is able to leave behind his personal faults and become noble in every tone and gesture when he takes a part calling for nobility, indicates that we also can exclude temperamental tendencies, at least during the time we are visualizing ideas.

Identifying yourself with ideas is the quickest road I know to good expression. Plato said, "What thou seest, that thou beest." To me this is exactly what visualizing is, seeing something to the exclusion of everything else until nothing exists to you but the ideas you are seeing. At such times you are entirely free from self. You move out from the seeing of the idea and as a result listeners become unconscious of you as a person and think only of what you say or do. Through visualizing you reach your maximum in accomplishment and have the satisfaction which goes with this attainment.

Chapter 6

SPONTANEITY

Spontaneity belongs to the rare few who refuse to fall into the world's prescribed pattern and dare to speak and act with naturalness and freedom. As a rule children have it, but education has not seemed able to encourage this quality and many adults find themselves in set grooves of custom—grooves which constantly restrict them when they try to express themselves.

The one who retains his spontaneity is as refreshing as the mountain brook romping down the slope, leaping some rocks, encircling others, loitering in the cool deep pools, and breaking away again with added fervor as it hurtles over a self-made dam. No fears to hold it down and curb its joy with reason's prose of thought. And yet it adjusts itself to its surroundings with nicety.

But this selfsame water may flow through aqueducts, obedient to enforced restrictions. It hardly seems the same then, for there is no running song, no sparkle left. These disappear, as they do in man, when studied intellect says, "Go this way," and forces action to obey the will.

When you yield to ideas your expression is so effortless that you seem moved by a power outside yourself. Your words and actions come with the same ease as a smile, without conscious thought of how it is done. If you are speaking, what you say will be right for you, with your experience, at this particular time, and you will enjoy saying it. You will speak as Bing Crosby sings. It is truly said of him, "He laughs at effort." So can you if you choose to let ideas direct you.

Spontaneity makes the plainest person interesting. Freedom, alertness, naturalness, a relish for what you are doing, give a

"pick up" whenever you come in contact with them. There is
a Pied Piper quality about spontaneity. It attracts. This is important to you, both in business and socially.

But its deadly imitation, effervescence put on from the outside in an effort to be popular, falls flat because it obscures the
natural graces.

Be yourself.

Don't be like the little mouse in an animated cartoon. He
watched the birds enviously as they flew about. Suddenly a good
fairy appeared and offered him one wish. He immediately
wished that he might have wings. No sooner said than he found
himself swooping about with great glee, but soon tiring of this
and wanting company he found that the birds were afraid of
him, the mice wouldn't play with him because they thought he
was puffed up, and when he sadly crawled into a cave with the
bats, they sang,

> You're nothing but a nothing, a nothing, a nothing,
> You're nothing but a nothing. You're not a thing at all.

That is what happens if you imitate others. Have the integrity
to "be yourself."

The lazy thinker, without realizing it, constantly imitates because he doesn't bother to get to the idea back of his activity.
He even imitates the way he has expressed himself on previous
occasions. Thus we hear a salesman giving his sales talk glibly
but without thought. We hear a lecturer, a minister, a reader,
imitating his planned presentation, not letting it be newly born
each time he gives it. Regardless of how often certain things need
to be repeated, always approach them with fresh interest. Use
the same method as the experienced actor who makes every
performance seem to be the only time the incidents of the play
ever happened, even when he has been in the same production
for three years. As Jane Cowl said, "The thought behind a part
must be gone through at each performance if there is to be il-

lusion and freshness, for it is from the thought that it stands for, that the word takes wings."

A mother who had dropped into the habit of constantly remonstrating with her children, suddenly realized that they paid no attention to what she said. In one of my classes it was pointed out to her that when you say a thing from habit instead of from inspiration, the idea is not helping you, and your words lose their authority. As soon as she restrained herself from speaking without thought and took time to listen to the idea back of her words, the children began to pay attention to her and obey. Habits are bad, even good ones, because they stop spontaneity.

Value your own findings and tell things the way they look to you, even though what you say or do may deviate from general opinion. We all have a different outlook. I see it from my side, you from yours. Perhaps no one has ever seen it the way you do. If you give your own viewpoint, you will speak with authority. We like firsthand information. This one utterly honest, spontaneous act of expressing something as you see it, is more convincing than hours spent in telling what others have written and said on the same subject, however well they may have expressed themselves.

Thoreau saw that we must not only be ourselves but let others around us be themselves. He said, "If a man does not keep pace with his companions, perhaps it is because he hears a different drummer. Let him step to the music which he hears, however measured or far away." A writer working on a book containing a new educational discovery went to an experienced teacher of writing for help. The subject matter was unique and challenging and the teacher became drawn into the task and began to impose his own views instead of confining himself to instructions on writing. After a few weeks of effort the author laid the book aside, completely discouraged. He had lost the inspiration of the idea and had no impetus to carry him on. But because the idea was so dynamic, eventually he was drawn back to his writing and the book was published. This incident shows how important it is for anyone in a position of influence to encourage those around him to "step to the music which *they* hear."

Look at some of these antonyms of spontaneity. Then look at the synonyms and see which group you want to line up with.

SPONTANEITY

downtrodden	sovereign
in harness, henpecked	independent, self-reliant
slave to	self-governed
necessity	free will
unwilling	with pleasure
grudgingly	with alacrity
premeditated	extemporaneous
calculated	natural
forced	freely
astral influence	self-determination
reasoning	knowing by intuition
studied	inspirational
impulsiveness	presence of mind

"The mass of men lead lives of quiet desperation," Thoreau also wrote. Why do they? I believe it is because they have lost their spontaneity, their enthusiasm for contemplated projects, their relish for what they are doing, their willingness and courage to express themselves. Frequently the fear of failure is so strong that men stifle the natural urge to expression, and remain silent. This negative attitude restricts growth. What can compare with the satisfaction which comes as you support a project or launch out into a new field of activity. Even though your effort does not immediately accomplish what you hope, you learn from the experience and as a result will express yourself better next time.

A woman painter who could never talk before a group, after studying this science of expression, found that she could break the lifelong inhibition, appear in the capacity of president for a large organization of painters, and even give lectures showing traditional artists how they could break away from their limiting conceptions of art. Although she is not young in years, the spontaneity of her outlook and the youthful happiness which shines in her face shows that, whatever our years, we do not need to "lead lives of quiet desperation."

Reading aloud is spontaneous when it has the zest and naturalness of conversation. This may not seem important to you, but unless you know how to read this way, you cannot hope to give listeners the full meaning. Unless you are able to look at printed words, to let them carry you to the ideas which inspired the author, and to read them as if you were talking, you need training; that is, you need to learn how to slight certain words and syllables, lengthen and intensify others, and most important of all, how to think of the meaning back of a word in the split second you say the word. A careful study of Part II will help you to do this, to make your reading of reports, directions, speeches, literature, as vital as your speaking. You will grasp more of the meaning in silent reading. Familiar words take on new significance when they are read with spontaneity.

One student who read aloud a great deal in his work, was complimented upon his fine reading and urged not to take lessons for fear they would destroy his naturalness. His reply was, "My reading was very poor when I began this work. It was only after I took lessons that I was able to make it sound as natural and convincing as if I were speaking my own thoughts."

The speaker who is spontaneous holds attention. His own glow of interest spreads like the ringed ripples from a pebble dropped into the water, until it takes in all that are within the radius of his voice. Listeners half asleep are brought to immediate attention by spontaneity.

To summarize:

Spontaneity—that instant response to the inspiration of ideas

—keeps your activities fresh and varied, your voice young, your reading conversational and convincing, your speech full of life.

We clarify too much and enjoy too little.
—FRANK LLOYD WRIGHT

Never imitate. Your own gift you can present with the cumulative force of a whole life's cultivation; but of the adopted talent of another, you have only an extemporaneous half-possession. That which each can do best, none but his Maker can teach him.—EMERSON

Habits are first cobwebs, then cables.—SPANISH PROVERB

That virtue of originality that men so strain after is not newness, as they so vainly think; it is only genuineness; it all depends on this single faculty of getting to the spring of things and working out from it.—RUSKIN

A turtle makes progress only when it sticks its neck out.
—ANONYMOUS

Life is being wasted. The human family is not having half the fun that is its due, not making the beautiful things it would make, and each one is not as good news to the other as he might be, just because we are educated off our natural track. . . .
Be game—take a chance—don't hide behind veils and veils of discretion. The spirit of youth should be in the young. Don't try to be ponderous. Youth has clear eyes. Let your colors be as seen with clear eyes. Go forward with what you have to say, expressing things as you see them. You are new evidence, fresh and young. . . .
It takes a tremendous amount of courage to be young, to continue growing—not to settle and accept.—HENRI

Chapter 7
RHYTHM

When you are full-charged with an idea—so much so that you are completely engrossed in it and forget yourself entirely, you move with its rhythm as you express it and what you do takes on an indefinable rightness.

I remember a New Zealand girl in one of the classes who illustrated rhythm by showing us how the Maori girls swing the poi in their dances. With a makeshift poi, a "tiny ball on end of string," she hummed a Maori tune, twirling the poi and moving to its rhythm. The class was entranced at the beauty of the performance. The tightness which often characterized her expression disappeared as she moved with the rhythm of the idea, and in its place a natural elegance of movement appeared.

When I first ask a class to give examples of rhythm, I usually get answers such as the beating of the heart, the ticking of a clock, a metronome, and these coincide with many of the dictionary definitions. But Roget broadens this concept with such words as these:

RHYTHM

orchestration	NOT	every man for himself
cadence		monotone
lilt		heaviness
co-ordination		derangement
natural		artificial
fluent		forced
style		good enough
restraint		vulgarity
purity		adulteration

clarity	obscurity
ease	labored
simplicity	complexity
symmetry	awkward or distorted
the right word in the right place	words that dislocate the jaw

The students then find that rhythm exists everywhere—in the drip of the rain, in a smooth-running engine, in the purposeful motions of a good stenographer, in the speech of a gifted and sincere statesman. It is in the breakers gliding smoothly in long straight lines, or heaping themselves riotously upon each other as they roll in, only to be drawn back firmly into the sea, from which they again escape and press shoreward. It is found alike in the chirp of a cricket or in the order of the universe by the one with eyes to see, ears to hear, and responsiveness to feel.

Rhythm includes style and timing—gifts which, many say, are unattainable if you are not born with them. It is true that rhythm cannot be gained through imitation or technique alone. It eludes the intellect's efforts to analyze it. You cannot merely reason it out.

But rhythm is within reach. It is inherent in an idea. So, to catch this rhythm, listen to the idea to the exclusion of everything else until you sense its very essence. Identify yourself with it. Then, because "what thou seest, that thou beest," you become that idea. At that moment you cannot help but have its rhythm in your speech, in your action.

Do not buck the rhythm of your times. Move with it and enjoy the forward march of progress. You do not have to accept everything new, but at least listen to the new and give it a chance to tell you what it has to offer. Don't approach it with a mind as closed as a clenched fist, full of "I don't like new things," "I don't approve of contemporary trends," "When I was young

. . ." Instead, move toward a new medium or experience with an open mind, free from prejudice but so alert that you penetrate to the core of the subject and are not fooled by that which is merely a fad and has no real merit.

Youth, not spoiled by pseudo education, is ready and willing to accept new rhythms. This kind of youth has nothing to do with years. It has to do with expectancy, spontaneity, relish, flexibility, courage, simplicity, expressiveness. Youth moves in rhythm. Age sets itself, is cautious, lives in the past, is blasé, refuses to yield to ideas. Again let me repeat that youth and age are qualities of thought, not quantity of years. Keep in the rhythm of your times and you stay young and continue to grow.

It is equally important to keep in the rhythm of your environment. For instance, upon visiting a new city, or organization, or household, or upon taking a new position, listen for the rhythm. Quietly feel it, let it direct you, and you will fit in unobtrusively. You become a part of it rather than an outsider; you feel at home. But when you enter a place carelessly or fearfully, or with self-centeredness, you break the rhythm. Things become stirred up, you irritate those around and you yourself often become tense and awkward because you are out of step with your surroundings.

I have found that I have a much richer experience when traveling if I do not go as a "Southern Californian," but efface my background and listen for the rhythm of each city I enter, get in step with my surroundings and enjoy what each place has to offer to the full, with no thought of comparison.

When speaking, as you fall into the rhythm of ideas, everything you say will follow in a direct line, relevant to your subject and properly correlated.

Rhythm in reading does not show itself in a chanting or singsong effect, regularity of accent and artificial inflection. It is the flow, the forward march of the selection. With it, words fall into their right relation to each other in beautiful continuity.

As rubato in music takes from one note to give to another because of their relative importance, so in reading, the meaning causes the reader to lengthen and intensify new-idea words at the expense of the unimportant or repetitious ones. But you lose this rhythm if you think of technique, of how you should read, or of your voice, or breathing.

For practice in identifying yourself with an idea, sometime try to experience the rhythm of a tree—any tree, a sycamore for example. Have a listening sense as you start. Let the tree talk to you. Enter into it gently. Do not push. You can seem to become the tree: to *feel,* as if it were your own, the strength of its great white trunk, the spread of its limbs out into the good air, the warmth of the sunlight on its leaves, the gentle releasing of an old leaf that it may slowly float down to the surface of the stream below, and its roots stretching deep, deep, down in their search for water and food, and to gain a balance for the gargantuan weight of its superstructure. Should you now describe it in any way—paint it or write about it—what you do would embody the tree's own rhythm.

Children readily catch an idea and fall into its rhythm. A good dance teacher makes them *see* the thing they are to "dance like," whether a dripping faucet, a robin, an opening flower, or whatever it may be. Children know this essence which is rhythm, but not all of them feel it the first time they try. This identification with the idea they want to express, can be learned.

This is the method an actor can use to "get into the skin" of a character. As he studies he is listening in every line of the play to penetrate better the innermost feelings of the person he is portraying. With intuitive perception he knows what this individual would do in certain situations, he can feel what his tones, his posture, his actions would be because he has entered into the rhythm of the character.

One actor told me that at times he attained a height in the first reading that he was never able to repeat. My explanation of this phenomenon is that, at the first reading, he had felt the rhythm of the character through inspiration, without his reason injecting into his thought the way others had taken the part, or the technique ordinarily used to portray certain emotions. He had not digressed from the intrinsic rhythm by wondering whether he should read it this way or that.

It is a great art to preserve the first inspiration and still perfect the technique, which must be done. No leaving the performance to chance. The real artist knows exactly what he is going to do and how he will do it.

If you could but reach the essence of an idea and stay with it, you could spontaneously have free expression; but you usually require practice before you can perfect an art, a profession, or a sport—in other words, before you can attain its rhythm and continue with it throughout your performance.

There is, of course, "beginner's luck," when in the first flush of interest and inspiration, one spontaneously surpasses the master. But this can seldom last. As a rule hours of thoughtful practice, to help you focus on the idea, keep your eye on the ball and not look where you are going to put it, precede a consistently good performance. A teacher gives varied approaches to his subject so that the pupil may find one approach that leads him to the underlying idea, knowing that once the student grasps that, he will have no more difficulty in his expression. Have you not heard a sportsman exclaim after many attempts to perfect a technique, "Oh, now I see! How easy!" He has finally fallen into the natural rhythm of the idea. Technique can be forgotten as long as he continues in that rhythm, but it should be renewed whenever his vision becomes dimmed.

The following incident illustrates how these two, technique and rhythm, may be reconciled. An actor asked the director of a play, "What did I do as I received that dreadful letter? It felt exactly right, but I don't know what I did." The director had not noticed. He was asked to see if he could catch the actor's natural reaction in a future rehearsal. After two or three rehearsals, the director said, "That time you caught hold of the back of the chair." "That's it! It felt right too!" the actor exclaimed. Then after inspiration had directed the action, he experimented as to the best way to make the gesture and then practiced until he had perfected it.

Nazimova listened until she found the rhythm of every scene, "not only of sound and movement, but of pause and thought, especially thought." She said the slightest slowing up or speeding up at the wrong time would destroy the rhythm. She also claimed that once the pattern was established, she followed it absolutely in each performance. There is one best way to do everything. It only appears when you move out from the seeing of the idea. But when you do that you give an unvarying performance. This does not mean thoughtless imitation each time, it means letting the underlying idea motivate your words and actions. There is a great difference in the two.

Self-will stops rhythm. It does not permit the idea to express itself in its own way. But when you have a humble thought, you yield to an idea and it controls every minute detail of your expression. It determines what you say and how you say it. It controls the breath, the pitch and coloring of the voice, the inflection, the gestures and action. It is irresistible. A harmonious adjustment of all the parts joins them into one related whole, that of service to the idea. Your expression becomes so impersonal that you may even catch your breath at its beauty, as if it were spoken by someone else.

A real artist has this rhythm—a freedom that is almost abandonment, balanced with a beautiful control. What he does is imitated without success by one who has not learned that rhythm must come from within and cannot be put on as an external.

The seventeenth-century Japanese drawing "Shrike" is done with a few deft strokes but still gives the feel of a season and the character of a bird. Only by identifying himself wholly with his subject could Myamoto Niten give the rhythm of the scene with this elegant simplicity. Japanese artists like to live for several seasons in a country before they attempt to paint it.

Horowitz, who in youth reached the top as a great technician on the piano, became a genius as he found that technique was not enough, that he must enter into the heart of the music and feel its rhythm and let it flow into his playing. It has been written of him that his aim is to make every phrase sing. The inexpressible beauty and appeal of delicate and melodious passages distinguishes his rendering from that of others whose principal attention is focused on the technically difficult parts. I shall never forget the sweetness and pathos of the song in Chopin's Funeral March as Horowitz played it. I was seated on the platform because the hall was filled and I saw him come on—a shy little man acknowledging the applause reluctantly. He sat down at the piano and seemed to quiet himself and the audience with his listening—his effacing of self and focusing on the idea, the music. Then the music came with the purity of the thing itself—not an approximation. I could see his face from where I sat. It was fierce—fierce with devotion to the idea and determination that nothing should interfere with its expression. He was a giant now. The rhythm of the idea swept those keys using every part of the man who had identified himself with the music.

This rare quality which makes him different from so many musicians, he attributes to personality. But it is his ability to efface his personality, to listen to and value the essence of the music, to be in empathy with it, and move out into its expression motivated by the very rhythm of the idea, which is his genius.

PART II

READING ALOUD—AN AID TO BETTER SPEAKING

Chapter *8*
THE FIRST STEP

While the theory you have just completed could be used as a basis for improving any of your conscious activities, this book focuses it on expression through the spoken word. The first step in this study is to learn to read aloud. Aside from the satisfaction which this accomplishment will give you, reading aloud is excellent preparation for learning to speak effectively.

1. It accustoms you to the sound of your own voice and makes you less self-conscious when you speak.
2. While reading you can improve your pronunciation and enunciation.
3. Assurance comes with the discovery that reading aloud is based on laws that you can master, and carry over into your speaking.
4. Most important of all, it teaches the timing of speech— that "eye-on-the-ball" quality which is the secret of holding attention either when reading or speaking.

Few realize the difference between their reading and their conversation. Reading has been considered mere expertness in pronouncing words distinctly and consecutively, with a certain amount of personal interpretation—something anyone could do. Or it has been taught in an artificial manner, filled with rhetorical pauses, studied inflections, conscious breath control, affected tones. As a result most reading is far removed from the natural way in which one talks.

In reading, because there is a written text, it is possible to keep up a steady flow of words and still not think of their significance; whereas in speaking one must keep his mind ever on what he wants to say, so that he may choose the right words to express his meaning. If reading is to have the same vigor as conversation, it must preserve this timing, so we come to the first, the foremost rule for reading aloud:

Think of the meaning of the word at the instant you say it.

When reading to yourself, you look at the subject matter and if it represents thoughts which you understand, it should carry you through to the same ideas which inspired the author to write them. In reading aloud you should read as though to yourself, except that you speak the word just as you think it, *not as an afterthought.*

To look at written words and speak them as fresh, new ideas —as though you were voicing your own thinking—brings into view all the beauty and power of the ideas they represent, and can be as thrilling as music interpreted by a great artist.

On the other hand, the usual way of reading—glancing ahead at as many words as possible and trying to determine their import, giving them out to the listener and at the same time looking ahead to see what comes next—cannot possibly bring out the full meaning. When thought is divided in this way, the interpretation is limited, the tone dead. *What you see when you say the word gives the voice its color.*

In fact I shall go further than this and say that the thinking is as important to the reader as paint is to the artist. No artist would make beautiful strokes with his brush without using paint. It is obvious that he would have no picture when he had finished. But few readers realize that a word spoken without thought, no matter how clearly enunciated, is as useless as a brush stroke without paint. Let me repeat that the thinking is as important to the reader as paint is to the artist.

Focusing on each new-idea word as you say it brings life and realism into the reading. You already use this timing in conversation; you can easily apply it to your reading. Its early

mastery depends on how soon you fully realize that it cannot be
put on from the outside, but is entirely dependent on your deep
and timely thinking.

To test your ability to apply this method, read the 23rd Psalm
aloud the way you usually have heard it read.

> The Lord is my shepherd; I shall not want.
> He maketh me to lie down in green pastures: he leadeth
> me beside the still waters.
> He restoreth my soul: he leadeth me in the paths of
> righteousness for his name's sake.
> Yea, though I walk through the valley of the shadow of
> death, I will fear no evil: for thou art with me; thy rod
> and thy staff they comfort me.
> Thou preparest a table before me in the presence of
> mine enemies: thou anointest my head with oil; my cup
> runneth over.
> Surely goodness and mercy shall follow me all the days
> of my life: and I will dwell in the house of the Lord for
> ever.

Did your reading sound as if you were speaking to someone?
Or did you intone the words so that their effect was somewhat
like this:

Incorrect: The Lord is my shepherd I shall not want.

Repeat the word *shepherd* using the rising inflection.

"Shepherd." Do you think of the meaning of the word when
you say it this way? You can't. Both you and the listener follow
the bend of the voice, reach for what is coming next, and do
not stay mentally with the word long enough to visualize the
ideas contained in this figure of speech. What is the significance

of the word to you? In *Roget's Thesaurus, shepherd* is grouped with *manager, leader, guiding star, adviser, pilot, lawgiver.* A shepherd protects his sheep, provides for them in all kinds of weather and in every location, reassures them when they are frightened. Thinking of these aspects of the word, say it again. "Shepherd." Now you have the coloring of the thought in the word and you will not sing it.

In pure reading, each word introducing a new thought should be said with a straight, positive tone.

To define this tone to yourself, give an adjective aloud to describe the weather: "Dull." "Sunny." "Threatening." This eye-on-the-ball tone is a "must" in both reading and speaking, if your words are to interest, arouse or move listeners to action.

Now go back to the 23rd Psalm. Pick it up as if for the first time. Suppose it to be a precious manuscript just unearthed and you are eager to find out what it contains. Say to yourself, "What are these words going to tell me?" Then listen.

As you read it aloud point to each new-idea word, focusing all your attention on it. Guard against thought-wandering; do not let it run ahead to see what is coming next, but see and feel something with each significant word.

The aim of the markings used in the following transcriptions is to prevent you from falling into mistakes common to reading aloud, and to help you bring out the full meaning of the words when you read.

The key to the transcriptions is on pages 235-37.

Questions stimulate thinking. Ask yourself:

What is this about?	The Lord
What about him?	is my shepherd
What does that mean to me?	(I shall not) want.

Why?   (He) maketh (me) to lie down
                                        (in) green pastures:
                                        As you say lie down *see it happen*

                                        (He) leadeth (me) beside (the)
                                        still waters.

                                        (He) restoreth (my) soul:
                                        Be careful not to stop thinking as you
                                        say the last word, soul.

                                        (He leadeth me in the) paths (of)
                                        righteousness for his name's sake.

The fourth verse is usually read with a rising inflection on all of the words which are marked.

Incorrect: Yea, (though I) walk (through the) valley (of the) shadow (of) death (I will) fear no-o-oh evil: for thou art (with me).

The following gives the correct pattern of this verse.

Correct: Yea, though I walk through the valley of the shadow of death, (I will) fear no evil: for thou are with me.

Be careful not to *hit* the words which are marked. Many readers feel that they bring out the meaning by exaggerated emphasis. Instead, value the meaning of the word as you say it and this will take care of its intensity.

The slighting of words in conversation gives a natural highlight to that which is important. One of the great faults in reading aloud is the failure to shorten unimportant words. The transcription already quoted is given below, with these words shown in parentheses.

Correct: Yea, though (I) walk through (the) valley (of the) shadow (of) death, (I will) fear no evil: (for thou art) with (me).

When you say *yea,* think of nothing but the positive idea of that word. See this and your tone will be direct and strong; you will not sing it. The next word, *though,* means *even if, admitting that.* Value the vowel sound in it. *I* is not stressed, for it means everyone, not just me. Valuing personal pronouns limits the application of the subject matter. *Walk* is an action word. See it happen as you say it. *Through* is important. It is different to walk *through* the valley than it is to walk *into* the valley. When reading *valley* you might visualize certain thought qualities, not merely a material valley. No one can tell you what to see, but be sure you see some usable idea consistent with the word simultaneously with the saying of the word. This is the only way to have color in your reading. *Shadow* is significant. *Death* is the high point in the phrase. Say it positively, not with bated breath. *Fear* is valued. *No* adds nothing until you find out, no what? No *evil.* Negatives are only valued for contrast.

After studying these transcriptions, reread the verse thoughtfully. Do you see more meaning as you read it this time? If not, start with, "What do these words say?" and listen as you read it again.

You may find that you are not able to focus on the word you are saying. Most people are double-minded in this respect, thinking of their ability or inability, of the listeners, or of what they will read next. It takes careful self-disciplining to get out of this habit, but it is essential in both reading and speaking.

At first you may have to read slowly in order to get the full substance. Hold yourself down until you are sure you are visualizing each important word as you say it. Soon, if you persist with this practice, the rhythm of the idea will bring the right tempo into your reading.

Several difficulties will present themselves at once. First is the problem of overcoming the constant temptation to look ahead and see what is coming next, instead of putting full attention on the thought of the moment. You may say, "How can I know what expression should be given to a word or phrase when I do not know what is coming next?"

You were advised to listen before you start with this reading. You will remember that in order to listen you must become mentally quiet, but also alert and attentive, not with strain, but with interest. This is not a casual happening. It is an accomplishment. When you are mentally listening for ideas as you read, you open the door for the real meaning of the words to come into thought, and this in turn, determines how they are read.

And you may also object: "Every word in a sentence should not have the same stress. Some are far more important than others. Won't they all sound the same if I am thinking only of the word I am saying?"

If you are 100 per cent on the word you are saying, really aware of its meaning, you unconsciously feel the *new-idea* words as they come, and give them proper value without a figuring-out process. Your undistracted interest makes you remember what has already been introduced and therefore should be unstressed, also what is new and needs emphasis. This focused valuing of each word takes care of the required differentiation in tone.

"But," you protest, "surely the rhythm would be lost if I think of one word at a time. There would be breaks between the words. The reading would sound choppy."

Not at all. If you are instant in your valuing of each word, not looking away mentally but placing the words side by side with a clear-cut nicety, as pearls on a chain, no spaces between them, each will be in its right place. There is a cohesion to an idea that holds the words together as a chain does the pearls.

Be careful not to be lazy in your reading. Apathy will break the rhythm; if you are inattentive, you do not grasp the depth of meaning. Self-indulgence causes you to linger over words or ideas which you particularly like, at the expense of others of equal importance. This gives a personal interpretation. The reader has no right to this indulgence. He should be at the service of the ideas. Only by using self-discipline in your reading will you have the right rhythm for the selection.

"Why do you use the Bible for examples?" is a frequent query. "The Bible is very different from anything I shall ever be reading."

The Bible is used for several reasons: A copy of the King James Version of the Bible is usually easy to procure. Its supreme literary value makes it excellent for reading practice. William Lyon Phelps has called it "the most beautiful monument ever erected with the English alphabet." So much meaning is in so few words that one or two lines of the Bible will illustrate a law of reading better than a whole page of most other texts. Also nothing needs a fresh approach in reading more than the Bible, long overlaid with dogmatic interpretations and emotionalism. It has been chanted, moaned, sung, preached, invoked, and when you start to read it you unconsciously fall into these mannerisms, unless you have a good grasp of the science of reading. If you can learn to read the Bible correctly, you will have the key to all reading.

In acting classes, Ethel Barrymore chose the Bible as a textbook for her students. She said its beauty and cadence are a stern test of voice and expression, that all who act should read the Bible, both for its depth of feeling and for its simplicity.

A stage producer in Hollywood stated after listening to one of my classes which was reading the Bible: "I always try out prospective actors with Shakespeare. Modern dialogue carries itself along and doesn't require the alert, intelligent thinking which Shakespeare demands. He always uncovers shallowness in a reader. The Bible, I can see, is an even greater test."

Chapter 9
GOOD CONVERSATIONAL STYLE

Listen to a round table discussion by some of our eminent men and women of letters and you are nearly always certain to hear good conversational styles of speech. The way these cultured persons express themselves when they are interested, involuntarily follows a pattern. Notice how they lengthen accented syllables, slight unaccented ones, and give value only to those words which are vital to the meaning. Notice their inflection and timing. Their conversational style is simple, convincing, direct, and has natural rhythm.

Although they slight many syllables and words, their speech is not slovenly. Neither is it pedantic—a fault too often heard in the speech of those striving for correctness. It is praiseworthy to seek to improve, but overprecise and stilted speech is as much a sign of ignorance as is the other extreme.

To be conversational does not necessarily mean to be casual. On the contrary, conversational style is just as suitable for the profound subject as for the humorous anecdote. Impressiveness must come from the depth of the thought expressed, not from any unusual manner of reading or speaking. For serious subjects the quality of tone will be that used in earnest conversation. Even on formal occasions the diction should not leave its informal pattern, although the tempo may be slower and fewer contractions may be used.

It has been mistakenly thought that a formal occasion calls for a formal style of speech. Webster defines *formal* in part as "conventional . . . punctilious . . . precise, starched, affected, stilted; outward, superficial." Is there ever a time when we want this kind of presentation? In the excellent foreword of *Webster's*

New International Dictionary, second edition, Professor Henry Cecil Wyld of Oxford University is quoted as saying, "As a matter of fact, the platform or pulpit pronunciation of the best public speakers hardly differs from that of the home circle."

Most persons wish to be unaffected and natural. Yet how few read aloud as if they were speaking. In reading "He gave them a black and white cat," we probably will hear each word given full value, while in talking the sentence would sound like this: "He gave th'm (a) black 'n' white cat."

The reason for this unnaturalness in reading is that *people do not know how they speak.* Most of us have not been taught to read as we speak. As a result we have fallen into these unnatural habits of pronunciation and emphasis. Fortunately, through recordings of speech, through television, talking pictures, and the work of discerning teachers, we are beginning to learn the laws which underlie the pattern of conversation in English. These laws, both of conversational pronunciation and of conversational reading, show us how we talk. By following them we can read as naturally as we speak.

Chapter 10

CONVERSATIONAL PRONUNCIATION

In conversation we unconsciously pronounce words differently than we do when the word stands alone. This difference is what we mean by conversational pronunciation—it shows in a shortening of unimportant words and syllables, a lengthening and intensifying of others. It is important to the reader that he understand this natural rhythm of speech, for he must use this pronunciation if he would have his reading sound as natural as his speaking.

Because the neutral vowel sound is substituted so frequently for other vowel sounds in conversation, I shall at times use the symbol, schwa (ə) when referring to it. Dictionaries mark this sound in different ways. Be sure to understand how it is symbolized in the one you use.

A common mistake is always to give the stressed form to the articles *the* and *a*. They are usually unstressed. *The* should have a neutral vowel, schwa, before a consonant sound, thə; a long *e* before a vowel sound, thē—thə hand, thē arm. The article *a* is always the neutral vowel sound unless *one* is its meaning. Should you ask for a match and be given a box of matches, you might say, "I wanted ā match," but in other uses give it the schwa sound.

It is not necessary to strain for a clear *t* sound and a long *u* in saying *nature*. Rather does the *t* have a *ch* sound. No one tries to keep the *t* sound in *righteous*. It is pronounced *ri'chas*. It is quite all right to use the *ch* sound with *lecture, literature, virtue,* and many similar words.

63

D often takes on a *j* sound, as in *soldier*. Examples of this are *verdure, education*. These *ch* or *j* sounds must not be stressed but should be kept very short and inconspicuous. Webster indicates them with a tie-bar, t͡u, d͡u.

Foremost in importance is the use of full, pure vowel sounds in the accented syllables, and short, obscured vowels in the unaccented syllables.

The unaccented syllables are obscured in three ways: The vowel sound takes on the short *i* sound, as in *image* (im′ij), the neutral vowel sound, as in *about* (ə bout′), or drops out altogether as in *evil* (ev′l). In the following lists the unaccented vowel changes to a short *i* sound.

village	vil′lij	carriage	car′ij
furnace	fur′nis	senate	sen′it
intimate	in′ti mit (not verb)	express	iks press′
climate	cli′mit	exact	ig zact′
always	al′wiz	effect	i fect′
Monday	Mon′di	employ	im ploy′

In final unaccented syllables the sound varies from short *e* to short *i*, but should not be toward the short *u*.

streamlet	stream′lit	brethren	breth′rin
heedless	heed′lis	(Brethren is often mispro-
roses	ros′iz	nounced as if it had three
started	start′id	syllables, breth-er-in.)

In the following lists, the vowel that is italicized has a neutral vowel sound. This sound is the same as the final *a* in *sofa*. To use the accented sound in these words is stilted, as to say ăb-surd.

*a*b hor′	va′c*a*nt	di′*e*t	*o*f fend′
*a*b surd′	break′f*a*st	an xi′ *e* ty	*o*c cur′
*a*b bre′vi ate	*e*s tate′	c*o*m pact′	pos sess′
loy′*a*l	clar′ *e*t	c*o*n form′	

Refer to a good dictionary until you become familiar with the correct sounds for the unaccented syllables in different words. Observe how good speakers deal with them. You probably are using the correct form in your speech. Soon your ear will accustom you to the conversational form and you will use it in your reading as well as your speaking.

The foreword of *Webster's New International Dictionary,* second edition, unabridged, written by John S. Kenyon, is excellent for a better understanding of conversational style.

Before final *l* and *n* the vowel is sometimes dropped out altogether.

eaten	eat'n	lesson	les'n
garden	gard'n	model	mod'l
evil	ev'l	vessel	ves'l

At times, *l, m* and *n* are voiced and form a short syllable as in

people	pep'l	*not* pē pul
able	ab'l	*not* ā' bul
chasm	kas'm	*not* kas'um

In the accented syllables use strong vowel sounds, and it will be easier to have short, crisp unaccented syllables. This gives balance to a word.

Monosyllables that are unimportant in their use should be unstressed—their vowels shortened and obscured. Say the sentence, *The snake began to move to and fro.* Notice how differently you say the two *to's.* They are spelled the same, but the meaning causes one to be stressed while the other is unstressed. Say several combinations using *and* in its unstressed form. If you are natural in this practice, *boy and girl* becomes *boy an' girl; you and I, you 'nd I; spick and span, spick 'n' span.* You are correct in using abbreviated forms for all such unstressed monosyllables.

Nothing brands a speaker or reader as inexperienced more quickly than giving these weak forms full value. It is not difficult to use them correctly, our chief concern being that we keep them short and unaccented and do not let them become heavy by overemphasizing them.

Chapter *11*

LAWS OF CONVERSATIONAL READING

Ease in reading comes through the understanding of a few rules put into conscious practice. These rules are not arbitrary, but are drawn from an analysis of the way experienced speakers express themselves when they are conversing. Although there is variety in their style, basic fundamentals are observed by the best of them. When these fundamentals are defined and used in reading aloud, the reading becomes as convincing as conversation, and *as natural.*

Timing

Foremost in importance is the law of timing, introduced already in Chapter 8. *The reader should time his thinking to be on each new-idea word at the very moment of speaking it.*

This right timing brings the same power, ease and perfection to reading that it does to a tennis stroke that meets the ball at the exact, right moment.

Pauses

In reading, pauses are as important as the words themselves. Speech serves but to start the thinking. Thought moves on faster and more accurately in the pauses than is possible during the speaking. The Chinese put it aptly. " 'When the words cease, the meaning flows on.' By the use of the pause they obtain an inexpressible richness in calm and reposefulness. It leads the thoughts of the onlooker into the nonvisible—typified by Lao Tzu's illustration of the vessel whose utility depends upon its nonvisible hollowness." (*Guide-Posts to Chinese Painting,*

by Louise M. Hackney.) We might say the same of reading—
its utility depends upon its nonaudible pauses. In them the
spoken words crystallize.

*The length of the pause following a phrase shows the value
placed upon the thought.*

The casual receives little time; the profound requires substantial thinking spaces. These pauses permit the expansion of
thought initiated by the spoken word.

For the sake of experiment, read this verse as you ordinarily
hear it read:

> And I heard a great voice out of heaven saying, Behold,
> the tabernacle of God is with men, and he will dwell with
> them, and they shall be his people, and God himself shall
> be with them, and be their God.—REVELATION 21:3

Now reread it, breathing only at the transcription mark Λ .
During the pauses stay mentally with the idea just read. Appreciate it. Value it. (The dots indicate the relative lengths of
the pause.)

> And I heard a great voice out of heaven saying. . . ,ΛBe-
> hold. . , Λ the tabernacle of God is with men. . , Λ (and he
> will) dwell (with them). . . , Λ (and they shall be) his peo-
> ple. . . . ,$\Lambda$and God himself (shall be with them. . . .), Λ
> (and be) their God.*

Breathe after the pause—not before it.

Take a fresh breath as you start a new phrase. Each thought
and the pause following should be held together as a complete
whole. The listeners will continue to think with you about the
idea just given until you take a breath for the next thought.
In this way you can hold people with an idea for an incredibly
long time.

* Key to Transcriptions on pp. 235-37.

Pause at the author's punctuation.

Punctuation marks are used by the author to indicate phrasing. As a rule there are plenty of them to accommodate you with breathing places and it is not necessary to infringe by imposing your own.

Here are some verses often read incorrectly because the pauses are not made at the punctuation marks alone.

> And they came with haste, and found Mary, and Joseph, and the babe lying in a manger.—LUKE 2:16

Unless well-defined pauses are at the commas only, it sounds as if all three were in the manger.

> For he that wavereth is like a wave of the sea driven with the wind and tossed.—JAMES 1:6

This is frequently read as if punctuation were after *sea*. The meaning is changed. This does not say that he that wavereth is like a wave of the sea, but "is like a wave of the sea driven with the wind and tossed."

Reading becomes ponderous when the author's phrases are broken up with rhetorical pauses.

Pause perceptibly before direct discourse:

This allows the listener to adjust himself to the change of person. For example:

> And one of the company said unto him . . , Master, speak unto my brother, that he divide the inheritance with me. And he said unto him . . . . , Man, who made me a judge or a divider over you? (And he said unto) them . . . , Take heed, and beware of covetousness: for a man's life consisteth not in the abundance of the things which he possesseth.—LUKE 12:13-15

Try reading this once without pauses and you will see how important pauses are to visualization.

Pauses give reading a conversational character.

When the printed word is spread out before you, it is possible to read along with scarcely any breaks in the flow of words—and this is the way a large majority read. In talking, however, you usually pause perceptibly between thoughts. If reading is to be conversational, it will have the same natural pauses.

Pauses are essential for visualization.

Without pauses the reader cannot visualize clearly. He needs them so that the words just uttered stir his imagination until what they represent is as vivid as if present before him, instead of merely the symbol—the writing. Then, by his voice, he can bring the pictures or ideas into view for others.

Pauses allow the listener to grasp the meaning.

When a reader or speaker does not pause the listener is unable to reach the full depth of meaning in profound subject matter. Just as one idea begins to develop, another crowds in and he only half grasps any of the ideas because he is hurried away too soon. Often he becomes discouraged and confused and gives up trying to understand.

Visualizing brings the right length of pause.

Through clear valuing of the ideas that unfold from the written words, the reader has an unerring and automatic gauge for the length of a pause, but when he allows his attention to wander he loses this control. For the reader to go off on little mental side-expeditions of personal experience, for him to fear being dramatic if he pauses too long, or for him to allow a nervous disposition to hurry him—any one of these traits exposes a divided thought, not wholly dedicated to what is being read. The pauses are not empty spaces. They must be filled with thought. In the following transcription you will have to see this thing happening in order to pause correctly.

And a certain man was there, which had an infirmity thirty and eight years. When Jesus saw him lie, and knew that he had been now a long time in that case, he saith unto him . . . . , Wilt thou be made whole . . . . ?

The impotent man answered him . . . , Sir, I have no man, when the water is troubled, to put me into the pool: but while I am coming, another steppeth down before me . . . . .

Jesus saith unto him . . . . , Rise . . . , take up thy bed . . . , (and) walk . . . . . . And immediately the man was made whole . . . , and took up his bed . . , (and) walked.—JOHN 5:5-9

Pauses always seem much longer to the reader than to the listener. If most readers would double or more than double the time they usually give to a pause, they would be approaching the right length.

If two persons are reading aloud, alternating, close attention is needed in order to have the right lengths of pause between the readings. Fear makes one jump in too quickly, and pauses that are too long sound as if the reader has lost his place. Feeling the rhythm of what is read will regulate how long the pauses should be. They should be the same length as if only one person were reading, and should vary according to the context. If a reader changed from one book to another there would of necessity be a perceptible pause, even with only one person reading.

Pauses do not mean the slow saying of words.

Let the tempo of speaking the words be conversational. The pauses occur only *between ideas* and should not be confused with the dragging of words, which is tiresome and denotes a dull thinker rather than a deeply appreciative one.

Vowels

Value the vowel sounds.

It cannot be repeated too often that it is through the vowel sounds in a word that the life, the beauty, and the power of the idea appear. Full pure vowel sounds characterize good positive diction.

Of course, it is only in important words that you stay with the vowel sounds, and if these words have more than one syllable, it is only the vowels in the accented syllables which are valued.

Vowels may have as many variations as thought itself. Say "Ah!" as you would if you sank on a cool porch swing after a walk in the hot sun. "Ah!" Notice how you lengthen it; notice the thought quality. Now say it as you would to a baby about to touch a hot stove. "Ah!" Say it as you would if you put your hand into a bag, thinking it contained fine, firm apples and encountered slimy, spoiled ones. "Ah!" You will see the variety of tones which may come from the same sound.

Visualize through the underlined vowel sounds in the tender lines of John Masefield's poem, "The West Wind":*

> It's a warm wind, the west wind, full of bird's cries;
> I never hear (the west wind) but tears are in my eyes.
> For it comes (from the) west lands, the old brown hills.
> (And) April's (in the west wind), and daffodils.

Read many different selections, visualizing in this way. Nothing teaches you to visualize but doing it, just as nothing teaches you to drive an automobile but driving an automobile. See old familiar favorites unfold through valuing the vowels.

* From *Collected Poems* by John Masefield, Macmillan, 1923. Used by permission of the publisher.

Words which add a new thought and which begin with a vowel sound often need a slight attack to prevent them from being slurred into the preceding word.

When this is not done in the following transcription, *is able* can become *i zabel, above all, uhbuh vall, without end, withow tend.*

> Now unto him that is able to do exceeding abundantly above all that we ask or think, according to the power that worketh in us, (Unto him be) glory in the church by Christ Jesus throughout all ages, world without end.
> —EPHESIANS 3:20, 21

Do not let this accent be sufficiently noticeable to distort the rhythm.

To avoid hitting words that need emphasis, stay longer on the vowel sound in the accented syllable.

Do not try to bring out the meaning by any artificial means such as strong emphasis or a higher pitch of the voice. Instead visualize as you say the accented vowel. This will take care of variance of pitch and tone and you will not feel the need of putting anything on from the outside. *This is of utmost importance.*

Verbs

Value verbs.

They are the action words and give life to your reading. To give proper value to the verbs, see the action happen *as you read;* then the listener will experience it with you.

Value the verbs consciously in this selection:

Correct: For we know in part, and we prophesy (in part). But when
that which is perfect is come, then (that which is in part)

�shall be <u>done</u> <u>away</u>. When I was a child, I spake (as a
child), I <u>understood</u> (as a child), I thought as a child:
but when I became a <u>man,</u> I put away (childish things).

—I CORINTHIANS 13:9-11

Do not have a rising inflection with *know*. Usually, in reading this verse, people are so interested in seeing the idea of *that
which is perfect,* that they do not see the action, *is come.* In the
last thought of the verse, *put away* should be read as if it were
happening at the time. Often the reader sees *childish things* but
fails to see what you do with them—*put away childish things.*
Even make a gesture of putting something away from you as you
say these words, that you may feel and express the action of the
verb.

Rarely stress the verb "to be."

Its emphasis causes reading to sound personal, argumentative
or facetious. To say:

Incorrect: God <u>is</u> a Spirit.

implies that someone has said He is not, and you insist He is.
It becomes an argument instead of a fact. It should state:

Correct: God (is a) Spirit.

Sometimes a false sense of rhythm will cause you to give forms
of this verb emphasis, as in this sentence:

Incorrect: Color <u>is</u> and always <u>has</u> been in the beholder, not in the
rose.

This causes the important words to be slighted.

Correct: <u>Color</u> is and <u>always</u> has been <u>in</u> the <u>beholder</u>, <u>not</u> in the
<u>rose</u>.

Read these verses correctly, valuing them a word at a time,
instead of the way you have usually heard them read:

Then said the Jews unto him, Thou art not yet fifty years old, and hast thou seen Abraham? Jesus said unto them, Verily, verily, I say unto you, Before Abraham was, I am.

—JOHN 8:57, 58

In the last thought, instead of emphasizing *was,* see the idea *before.* "<u>Before</u> (Abraham was), <u>I am</u>,"

When action is predicted and then is completed, strong emphasis is given to the verb which relates the finished action.

This verb is stressed with a slightly downward inflection. To illustrate: He said, "Come in," and he <u>came</u> in.

And the Lord said unto him,⋀What is that in thine hand? And <u>he</u> said,⋀A rod. (And he said),⋀Cast it on the ground. And <u>he</u> <u>cast</u> (it on the ground), and it became a serpent; and <u>Moses</u> <u>fled</u> (from before it). (And the Lord said unto Moses),⋀Put forth thine hand, and take it (by the) tail. And he <u>put</u> forth his hand, and caught it, ⌐and it became a <u>rod</u> in his hand.—EXODUS 4:2-4

In the last example, where two words make up the verb, *put forth,* the effect of a downward inflection comes from emphasizing the first word and lowering the last one.

A right valuing of verbs prevents incorrect emphasis of prepositions.

Especially is it a tendency to stress *unto* and *upon.* For example, in Exodus 3:13, we frequently hear:

Incorrect: The God of your fathers hath sent me <u>unto</u> you.
Correct: The God of your fathers hath <u>sent</u> me unto you.

And in Psalms 145:15:

Incorrect: The eyes of all wait <u>upon</u> thee.
Correct: The eyes of all <u>wait</u> upon thee.

And in Matthew 11:28:

Incorrect: Come <u>unto</u> me all ye that labor.
Correct: <u>Come</u> unto me all ye that labor.

Of course, where there is a contrasting of prepositions, the contrast should be valued, as in Colossians 1:16:

> For by him were all things created, that are in heaven, (and that are in) <u>earth</u>, visible and <u>invisible</u>, whether they be thrones, or dominions, or principalities, or ⌐powers: all (things were created by him), and <u>for</u> him:

Introducing new ideas

Every word which brings a new thought should be introduced with a positive tone.

In this text such words are called "new-idea" words.

If you focus on the meaning when you read a passage, you will use a straight tone for each word that adds to the picture, valuing the vowel sounds in the accented syllables. Unimportant words drops out of sight, as they do in conversation. Practice on this verse.

> (For the) mountains (shall) depart, (and the) <u>hills</u> be removed; but my kindness (shall) <u>not</u> (depart from thee), neither (shall the) covenant (of) my <u>peace</u> (be removed), saith the <u>Lord</u> that hath mercy on thee.   —ISAIAH 54:10

Students have frequently been taught to hold the voice suspended at commas, dropping it at periods only. Actually, *the punctuation marks do not tell what to do with the voice.* Their purpose is to separate ideas. The meaning should determine the inflection.

Continuity

Continuity is defined in the *American Dictionary* as "a continuous or connected whole." In Webster's as "uninterrupted connection or succession; close union of parts; cohesion."

Reading must have continuity if one is to grasp the full significance of the text. It is often lost because readers are so busy saying the words distinctly that you "can't see the forest for the trees," you can't grasp the meaning for the words. Sometimes they give as definite emphasis to every syllable and final consonant as if they were pronouncing the words to be spelled. Chapters 9 and 10, which call attention to conversational style and pronunciation, can help a great deal in bringing continuity into reading.

We might illustrate continuity with a rose. If you dismembered it, each petal and part has beauty of form and color, but you really have no concept of the magnificence of a rose from merely viewing these parts. In a rose there appears a marvel of relationship. You do not think of it as a series of things but as one complete whole. All of each petal cannot be seen in the rose—neither should all of each word and phrase be heard in reading. Unaccented monosyllables and syllables should be slighted as much as they are in conversation, if you would hold the words of a sentence together with continuity.

However, it is not enough for you to read every sentence correctly. You must also feel the relation which the sentences and paragraphs hold to each other. This does not require a lengthy figuring-out process before you read. Alertness to the following law will dovetail the parts together into one related whole.

Continuity comes into reading when the new-idea words and phrases are visualized and introduced in a positive tone, and repetition of these words for the purpose of giving more information about them, is slighted.

In the following Psalm, parentheses are placed around the parts which are repetitious:

> Praise ye the Lord. (I will praise the Lord) with my whole heart, in the assembly of the upright, (and in the) congre-

gation. The works (of the Lord) are great, sought out of all
them that have pleasure therein. (His work is) honorable
(and) glorious: (and his) righteousness endureth forever.
(He hath) made (his wonderful works to be) remembered:
(the Lord is) gracious and full of compassion. (He hath)
shewed his people the power (of his works), that he may
give them (the) heritage (of the) heathen. (The works of
his hands) are verity (and) judgment, all his command-
ments (are) sure.—PSALMS 111:1-4, 6, 7

The repetitious parts are read without emphasis, often at a
lower level, at times a little more rapidly. You will automatically fall into the best way if you are listening for the meaning
and do not let your thought digress. Notice how this reading
holds the ideas together in their right relation to each other
and brings out the meaning intelligently.

As the reader is acutely aware of each new thought he introduces, it makes an indelible impression on him and he involuntarily gives it less value when it reappears, bringing out only
the new-idea words. That which has been read, not what is
coming, determines the emphasis. Then he is with the listener,
who cannot look ahead, and he will give full value to the present
instead of anticipating in his tone the next line of thought.

Giving less time to an idea which has already been introduced does not underemphasize it. You can satisfy yourself on
this point by reading the 13th Chapter of I Corinthians and
emphasizing the word *charity* every time it occurs.

Incorrect: Charity suffereth long, and is kind; charity envieth not;
    charity vaunteth not itself, is not puffed up.

Now reread it, introducing *charity* definitely the first time it
occurs. When it is in the parentheses say it thoughtfully but
not with emphasis.

Correct: Charity suffereth long, and is kind; (charity) envieth not;
    (charity) vaunteth not itself, (is not) puffed up.

LAWS OF READING   79

You will know more about charity after the second reading than
after the first.

There are occasions when ideas already have been introduced
and still need to be given much value. These are read on a lower
level and are given value by the tempo, but they are not introduced as a new idea would be introduced. An example of
this occurs in John 13:34,35:

> A new <u>commandment</u> I give unto you, that ye love one an-
> other; (as I have loved) you, that ye <u>also</u> love one <u>another</u>.
> <u>By this</u> ⌊shall all men <u>know</u> (that) ye are my <u>disciples,</u> if
> (ye have love one to another).

*When words are repeated for emphasis with no new idea
included, they are not slighted, but given greater intensity.*

We would not read, "Arise, (arise) . . ." But "Arise, arise . . ."
"Holy, holy, holy . ."

Do not lose last words.

You may share the common tendency to let down in pitch
and intensity with the last words. This happens because you
stop thinking before you reach them. Can you imagine Sir
Winston Churchill dropping his voice at the end of his statements? The letdown at the end of a sentence weakens the effectiveness of both speech and reading. Often the last word is the
most important. <u>The remedy is to *refuse to let go mentally until
you have completed the sentence.*</u> Think of the meaning of the
last word just as you say it. Bring your sentence up to a climax if
that word is vital to the idea. Do not let it be lost. This does not
mean to raise the pitch on the last word of every sentence. Many
radio and television announcers have fallen into this artificial
pattern to avoid losing last words.

In the following verse the last word is ordinarily slighted.

Incorrect: Be $\underset{\llcorner}{}$evil, but overcome $\underset{\llcorner}{}$good.
not overcome of   evil with

Correct: Be not overcome of evil, but overcome (evil) (with) good.
—ROMANS 12:21

Do not stress *with,* but *good.* The second *overcome* is stressed because it is contrasted to *be not overcome.*

This one law—to refuse to let go mentally until you have completed the sentence—will give vitality to what you read and aids in holding the listeners' unwavering attention.

Explanation of tone level transcriptions

That you may become conscious of the play of your voice as you express ideas, the inflections in certain familiar phrases are shown here. In these transcriptions the circles represent accented syllables, the dashes represent unaccented syllables, and the curves represent slides of the voice. The intervals are only comparative. This method will be used to illustrate the change of pitch when reading certain passages.

Oh?   I don't want to.   Where are you going?   Not me.

Questions

Only questions which can be answered by "Yes" or "No" should have a rising inflection on the last word.

Even these questions are stronger if the circumflex is slight. The effect of a question is given when the last word has a straight emphasis; the voice is not dropped, as at a period, nor raised. Try the following questions in this manner. Although they can be answered by "Yes" or "No," you will see that you give the sense of a question through a lack of inflection on the last word. "Are you going with me?" "Can you hear the music?"

In a question which cannot be answered by "Yes" or "No" there is no rising inflection on the last word. "What is your name?" "Where are you going?"

The two kinds of questions are illustrated in the following transcriptions:

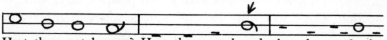

May I come in?   or   May I come in?   What do you want with me?

Either of the first two is correct but the second one, which has a straight rather than a rising tone on the last word, is more impersonal and stronger. No one would naturally say the last one with a rising circumflex but some, when reading aloud, will suddenly see a question mark and raise their voice on such last words, thinking that a question mark means "raise your voice."

In long questions, even though they can be answered by "Yes" or "No," when the desire is to inspire thinking rather than to receive an answer, it is better not to have a continual upward inflection, because it is not easy to visualize in this way.

Read the following verse the way you usually hear it read. See if you are not distinctly conscious of the bending of the voice rather than the meaning.

> Hast thou not known? Hast thou not heard, that the ever-
> lasting God, the Lord, the Creator of the ends of the earth,
> fainteth not, neither is weary? There is no searching of his
> understanding.—ISAIAH 40:28

To help you avoid this rising intonation, the word where you can change to a statement is marked with a downward inflection in the next transcription. Unless this is done, there will be an upward inflection with every word before a punctuation mark: God, Lord, earth, not, weary.

Hast thou not known? Hast thou not heard, that the everlasting

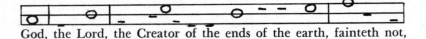

God, the Lord, the Creator of the ends of the earth, fainteth not,

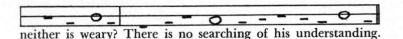

neither is weary? There is no searching of his understanding.

Here is another long question which can be answered by "Yes" or "No" and still can be visualized more clearly if a rising inflection is not continued throughout the verse. Try to read it correctly yourself and then check with the pattern.

> They that see thee shall narrowly look upon thee, and consider thee, saying, Is this the man that made the earth to tremble, that did shake kingdoms; that made the world as a wilderness, and destroyed the cities thereof; that opened not the house of his prisoners?—ISAIAH 14:16, 17

They that see thee shall narrowly look upon thee, and consider thee,

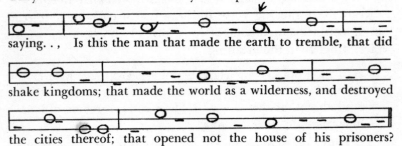

saying. ., Is this the man that made the earth to tremble, that did

shake kingdoms; that made the world as a wilderness, and destroyed

the cities thereof; that opened not the house of his prisoners?

In this transcription, the question is turned to a statement on the word *earth*. Even with these patterns it is difficult to get out of the questioning inflection. Say *earth* as if there were a period after it. This will probably give it the positive downward inflection which will stop the questioning slides in the rest of the verse.

Negatives

Do not stress negatives except when they make a contrast.

A tendency in reading is to emphasize all negatives at the expense of the descriptive words which should receive value. For example:

Incorrect: He that covereth his sins shall <u>not</u> prosper.

—PROVERBS 28:13

To stress *not* gives the listener nothing until he hears the idea *prosper*; and usually when the word *not* is stressed, the word *prosper* is lost.

Correct: He that <u>covereth</u> his <u>sins</u> (sh'll not) <u>prosper</u>.

The second thought of the 23rd Psalm is an example of a negative which is usually stressed.

Incorrect: I shall <u>not</u> want.

You really have no illustrative word until you come to *want*.

Correct: I shall not want.

In the verse following, *not* is used as a simple negative and also in a contrasting sense. See if you can read it correctly before you examine the pattern.

> While we look not at the things which are seen, but at the things which are not seen: for the things which are seen are temporal; but the things which are not seen are eternal.
>
> —II CORINTHIANS 4:18

Correct: While we <u>look</u> not at the things which are <u>seen</u>, but (at the things which are) <u>not</u> (seen): (for the things which are) seen (are) <u>temporal</u>; (but the things which are) <u>not</u> (seen) (are) <u>eternal</u>.

Comparisons

Comparison of two words or phrases shows only in the accent of the last member of the comparison.

An example is to say, "Asc̲ending and d̲escending." You would hardly say, "She was descending the stairs," but in the example the contrast justifies this change of accent. You do it unconsciously in conversation. Do not say, "A̲scending and d̲escending." The listener hears only one word at a time. This unusual pronunciation of the word *ascending* without any reason for it is startling, and you would not do it if your thought were wholly on the word you were reading. Your thinking has strayed ahead and is partly on the comparison. But if you introduce the idea *ascending* clearly, it is natural to make the contrast by means of the different accent in the last member of the comparison. Examples of this are *inbound* and *o̲utbound; mortals* and *i̲m-mortals; obtained* and *r̲etained.* "And be not confo̲rmed to this world: but be ye tra̲nsformed by the renewing of your mind."

Comparison of two phrases does not change the accent of any single word, but changes the emphasis of the words. In these, care should be taken to introduce the subject about which the comparison is to be made and not to think first of the contrast.

Incorrect: For to be carnally minded is death; but to be spiritually minded is life and peace.—ROMANS 8:6

You have a contrast but lose the vital word *minded.*

Correct: For to be carnally minded (is) death; but to be spiritually (minded) is life (and) peace.

The use of this law of contrasts is helpful in reading reports which involve comparative figures. Good visualizing will cause you to slight that which is repetitious, or too detailed for the listener to grasp, and to emphasize the important comparisons.

Income totaled $49,023.12 in 1955 as against only $41,644.75 in 1954, should be read: Income totaled <u>forty-nine</u> <u>thousand</u> (twenty-three dollars and twelve cents) in nineteen <u>fifty</u> <u>five</u> as against forty-<u>one</u> (thousand. . ᶠSix hundred forty-four dollars and seventy-five cents) (in nineteen fifty) <u>four</u>.

Reasoning words

Value reasoning words.

It helps listeners to think with the reader. Such words as *though, therefore, because, then, but,* etc. often have a message which requires that they be said thoughtfully. At the same time the rhythm must not be distorted by stressing them unduly or pausing after them. Practice this law in the following selections:

> For we are saved by <u>hope</u>: (but hope that is) <u>seen</u> is not hope: (for what a man) seeth, (why doth he yet) <u>hope</u> (for)? But (if we hope for that we see) <u>not</u>, then (do we with) patience wait (for it.)—ROMANS 8:24, 25

> Though I speak with the tongues of men and of angels, and have not <u>charity</u>, ᶠI am become as sounding brass, or a tinkling cymbal.—I CORINTHIANS 13:1

> I have set the Lord always before me: because he is at my right hand, I shall not be moved. <u>Therefore</u> my heart is glad, and my glory rejoiceth: my flesh also shall rest in hope.—PSALMS 16:8, 9

Reasoning words should not be hit or sung; they should be thought through as they are said. For instance, *though* may mean "even in the event that," *because*—"for the reason that," *therefore*—"as a result of this."

Direct address

When addressing a person directly and calling him by some identifying name, the mood of the speech is largely established by the inflection used as you say the name. When the mood is deferential, casual or friendly a rising inflection is used, as:

Simon Peter said unto him, Lord, whither goest thou?

In a command or when arresting attention, the direct address is given with finality, with a downward inflection. When Jesus was addressing the dead Lazarus, the Bible states that he cried with a loud voice, "Lazarus, come forth." If the name *Lazarus* is said with a rising intonation, it is impossible to feel the power which such a command would necessarily include. Positive inflection gives the effect of a loud voice.

The Bible, telling of the time Peter walked on the water to go to Jesus, says ". . . when he saw the wind boisterous, he was afraid; and beginning to sink, he cried, saying, Lord, save me" (Matthew 14:30). The arresting tone used here can only be shown with this downward inflection: Lord, save me.

When the mood needs to be impersonal use as little inflection as possible in the direct address. For instance in the following verse, John 17:5, use a straight tone at a lower level, for *O Father*.

And now, ˪O Father, glorify thou me with thine own self
with the glory which I had with thee before the world was.

In the Psalms are places where the direct address includes several phrases or clauses. These will sound sincere only as there is slight variation in the inflection. For example:

O Lord God, to whom vengeance belongeth; O God, to whom vengeance belongeth, shew thyself.—PSALMS 94:1

All of this verse is direct address except the last two words. This phrase is brought in at a higher level; the rest has a straight tone.

In these lines from *Renascence* by Edna St. Vincent Millay,

notice that unless the words *O* and *God* have equal stress, they
sound insincere:

> O God, I cried, no dark disguise
> Can e'er hereafter hide from me
> Thy radiant identity!*

Tempo

*Tempo should be determined by the ideas and by the circum-
stances under which they are read.*

Read the following selections, staying mentally with each new-
idea word, and notice the variation in tempo which comes without premeditation:

> Thus saith the Lord the King of Israel, (and his) redeemer
> (the Lord of) hosts . . . ; **S** I am the first, and (I am the) la**H**st;
> and beside me (there is) no God.—ISAIAH 44:6

Feel the different tempo that springs up as you read Sidney
Lanier's lines from *The Song of the Chattahoochee:*

> Out of the hills of Habersham,
> Down the valleys of Hall,
> I hurry amain to reach the plain
> Run the rapid and leap the fall,
> Split at the rock and together again
> Accept my bed, or narrow or wide,
> And flee from folly on every side
> > With a lover's pain to attain the plain
> > Far from the hills of Habersham,
> > Far from the valleys of Hall.†

If you realize the profound ideas in the Bible selection, you
are forced to read more slowly than you do in the flowing lines
of the poem. Experiment with different selections and you will

---

* *Renascence and Other Poems,* Harper & Brothers. Copyright, 1912, 1940, by
Edna St. Vincent Millay. Used by permission of Brandt & Brandt.
  † Used by permission of Charles Scribner's Sons.

see how the tempo is regulated as you time your thinking with the words which you read.

When addressing large groups you will automatically read more slowly than in ordinary conversation, just as you would if you called across a canyon to one on an opposite hill. However, avoid dragging words merely because you are speaking or reading from a platform or pulpit. Be spontaneous.

Timing and tempo are not identical as used in this book. *Timing* means thought on the meaning of the word at the instant the word is spoken. *Tempo* refers to the rate of speed used.

At first, self-consciousness may make you drag in your effort to focus on each new-idea word, but that will be overcome by thoughtful practice. You are learning the greatest art in speech —that of timing the thought to the spoken word. Many do it in conversation; few do it in reading.

The tempo of your reading is often influenced by the disposition. For instance, a judge in a speech class read very rapidly. He said that he did everything that way—that he was born that way. Yet when pauses between ideas were recommended, he said that in court you must pause to be sure the jury grasps what you say. It was brought home to him that it is as important to pause in reading as it is in court procedure, so that listeners can perceive the ideas expressed. Someone, justifying him, said, "Isn't it that he thinks rapidly all day and sees things quickly?" Would he want to hear his favorite symphony speeded up because he thinks quickly? He would be able to comprehend it intellectually, but he would lose the experience of the thing itself. Tempo should stem from the subject matter, not from the reader's disposition.

Fear also makes you hurry, and prevents you from giving full value to words and pauses. Equally bad is dragging the words. Only the quiet, alert thought will see the idea back of the words and use the right tempo.

Superlatives

Make a superlative superlative.

By saying it slowly you can visualize the extreme it represents. At times this calls for almost a syllabling of the words, as: <u>utter</u>-<u>most</u>, <u>great</u>-est, <u>farth</u>-est, <u>e</u>nds of the <u>e</u>arth. The time is taken on the vowels in the accented syllables, the unaccented syllables remain short, as in all conversational pronunciation.

Series

In a series, do not loop the different members together with a rising inflection.

The listener's thought follows the inflection of the voice. When it is a rising one it tends to make the listener feel, "This is nothing of importance," and reach for the next idea, not valuing the one being given. It is wrong to do this in any kind of reading, but it is especially noticeable in the reading of a series.

Incorrect: For I am persuaded, that

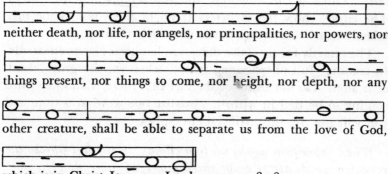

neither death, nor life, nor angels, nor principalities, nor powers, nor

things present, nor things to come, nor height, nor depth, nor any

other creature, shall be able to separate us from the love of God,

which is in Christ Jesus our Lord.—ROMANS 8:38, 39

As a result of this emphasis, the listener is not allowed to remain mentally on the important words and the thought is not clearly given.

Correct: For I am persuaded, that

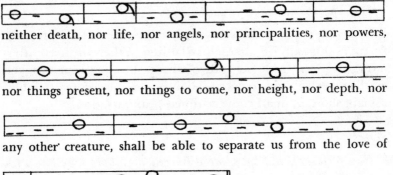

neither death, nor life, nor angels, nor principalities, nor powers,

nor things present, nor things to come, nor height, nor depth, nor

any other creature, shall be able to separate us from the love of

God, which is in Christ Jesus our Lord.

This reading-up habit causes you to fall into certain patterns. For example, consider the way in which a series of two or more words is read. With two words, many sing up with the first and down with the second, as: "full of grace and truth"; with three or more members in a series, they will read up with all but the last: "Thine is the kingdom and the power and the glory." The curves show the incorrect trend of the voice. Some mistakenly think this brings music into their reading.

The remedy for this false inflection has been given repeatedly. In reading "full of grace and truth," when you say *grace,* think of it alone. Do not think of the fact that there is another word coming to be tied in with it. Visualize one word at a time and you will not use this artificial circumflex.

When repetition works up to a climax, in the last phrase the repeated words are re-emphasized and read more slowly.

Example:

   . . . (and that) government (of the) people, by (the people), and for the people, shall not perish from the earth.

When a series of phrases or clauses work up to a climax, the climax is usually read more slowly—not dragged, but deeply valued.

Example:

Whither shall I go from thy spirit? (or whither shall I) flee (from thy) presence? If I ascend up into heaven, thou art there: (if I) make my bed in hell, behold, (thou art) there. (If I) take the wings of the morning, and dwell in the uttermost parts (of the) sea; even there shall thy hand lead me, and thy right (hand) shall hold me.—PSALMS 139:7-10

Are all apostles? (are all) prophets? F (are all) Teachers? are all workers of miracles?—I CORINTHIANS 12:29

Levels

New-idea words and phrases will each have their own individual pitch, tempo and intensity when the meaning behind them is seen as they are read.

This individualization cannot be done mechanically. Nothing is worse than to alter pitch merely for diversity. A sameness in tone indicates lack of distinct visualizing. Should this occur in your reading, go back and be sure you see the ideas behind the words as you read, and observe their relationship to each other; then the monotony will disappear. In building up to a climax you do not necessarily make the pitch higher in each member. Sometimes great emphasis and sincerity come with a lowering of the pitch on the climax. It must be visualizing which determines what the voice does, not reasoning nor premeditation.

In I Corinthians 13:7, Paul, in defining charity, says:

Beareth all things, believeth all things, hopeth all things, endureth all things.

Before illustrating the pattern of this verse, let me give you the way these words are defined from their original Greek derivations in Strong's *Bible Dictionary,*

> *Beareth:* to roof over, i.e., to cover with silence.
> *Believeth:* to have faith in, to credit. From a word meaning "reliance on truth."
> *Hopeth:* to expect or confide. From a word meaning "to anticipate with pleasure; expectation or confidence."
> *Endureth:* to undergo; to persevere.

Thinking of each of these meanings as you say the words they apply to, read the passage again. This time you will be sure to find variation in the pitch. It will read something like this:

> Beareth all (things), believeth (all things), **F** hopeth (all things), **S** endureth all (things). [H above a word = higher pitch, L = lower, F = faster, S = slower.]

In working on the reading of a selection composed of a series of words or phrases, it is helpful to number the different members of the series. This reminds you that there is to be a building up, and signals you not to overemphasize the first member so that it is impossible to show a climax. A verse from a poem by John Greenleaf Whittier illustrates this building up:

> We faintly hear, we dimly see,
> In differing phrase we pray;
> But, dim or clear, we own in Thee
> The Light, (the) Truth, the Way.

No attempt should be made to give a great change in pitch. The slightest variation in tone shows the difference between alive reading and dead repetition of words.

Visualizing causes words and phrases to be spoken at different levels, with varying intensity and tempo—causes reading to be real music.

Some mistakenly think they can bring this music into their reading by conscious slides in the voice. This is as unnatural as it would be to play every long note in a Beethoven sonata with a tremolo to give it more feeling. The music is in the sonata itself and needs no outside flourishes to enhance its beauty. So it is in reading. Inexpressibly sweet music is in an idea read according to the meaning, and there is no need to try to bring music in from the outside. So much rhythm, harmony, and melody are in ideas correctly spoken that they make a music of their own.

The People, by Carl Sandburg, was given in a recent college program. Groups danced the thought of each part to improvised music. But at times they danced to the spoken words alone, and it was a music more impressive than that of song or instrument.

Chapter *12*
NATURAL USE OF THE VOICE

You may think that you want a beautiful voice, a resonant voice, or a deep and convincing one, but your real need is to have a free voice. Then it will take on the quality of your thought at the instant you speak, and will vary from the gentle to the commanding, from the rich to the clear and strong, from the broad and impersonal to the warm and sympathetic. A free voice is a useful one and will always have natural beauty and resonance.

Observe a healthy baby. What is the technique that enables him to express his feelings so perfectly with his voice that his mother can tell from his cry whether he is angry, hungry or in pain? And he can change a lusty bellow to a gentle coo with no indication of a strained throat.

The secret of his splendid voice control is, first, an open throat which permits deep breathing; and second, his focus on what he is doing, which brings the right amount of breath to express each of his needs. He is not sidetracked from his purpose. When he cries, he cries from the top of his head to the tips of his toes. He breathes the same way—deep, rhythmic breathing. It is the lack of these two things which causes a voice to sound old. When the throat is partially closed by negative thinking or when the attention is not wholly on what one is doing, deep breathing is impossible and the result is usually an unpleasant voice. In-difference, instead of absorbing interest, keeps one from responding to the idea and expressing its qualities in the voice.

The throat should be as an open gate, its one business being to keep out of the way. You might think that this would be easy to do but almost any mental disturbance affects the throat. Look at our many figures of speech which illustrate this point: "A lump rose in her throat." "Her heart leaped into her mouth." "The words stuck in his throat." Each of these metaphors shows a sense of obstruction in the throat which impedes the freedom of the voice. On the other hand, the one who is habitually sincere, gracious, honest and unafraid usually has an open throat and an unconstrained voice.

Happily you do not have to wait until you have overcome all negative temperamental tendencies before you can have a free voice. An actor may have wonderful tones, not because he is a better man than others, but because he loses his prejudices, fears and personal feelings at the moment he speaks, and focuses on what he is saying. Then the thought quality appears in his tone, whether it be tenderness or hatred, fear or courage. You can use the same technique.

Breathing should be a natural and unconscious process, even when you are speaking or reading, and it will be if you focus on what you are saying and keep an open throat. It is not necessary to draw in air through the nose when you breathe, raising the chest and tensing as you do it. You will never see a healthy baby do this. Air comes into the lungs as easily as it does into a hot-water bottle when the stopper is out and you separate the two sides. You do not have to force it in. It comes because "nature abhors a vacuum." On the same principle when you want to say something, your valuing of the idea causes a pickup, an unconscious expansion throughout the body. Air constantly moves in to fill this space without your actually drawing a breath.

Put your hands on your sides, a little below the waist; relax the root of the tongue to open the throat and, without any consciousness of breath, say the vowels positively, each complete in itself, not looped together: A...E...I...O...U... If you have an open throat and are mentally focused upon what you are doing, your hands will feel an expansion with each sound. This is the same action which takes place in a hearty laugh, often called a "belly laugh" in show business. If your speech is as natural and wholehearted as your laugh, you will feel this same action. Don't make a muscular effort to cause the expansion. It must happen as a natural result of the speaking. The expansion which takes place with each sound brings the necessary air without conscious effort. Should you hold your breath this expansion cannot occur. But if you are easy and keep an open throat, you can go on saying the vowels indefinitely without taking a deliberate breath.

Feel that you are *in* breath, not trying to get it. Notice how the body tenses if you draw in a quick breath before speaking. This method causes a tight quality in the tone.

You take a breath automatically for everything you do when you are at ease. If you are going upstairs, you do not say, or think, "I am going upstairs; I must take a big breath," and accompany this statement with a vigorous indrawing of air. Instead, you simply think of going upstairs, and go, taking the right amount of air without thought.

But when you start to read or speak, you may make yourself tense by inhaling an abnormal amount of air. Breathe often in reading. Let fresh inspiration come as you start each phrase. The seeing of the idea causes a natural expansion. Do not go as far as possible on one breath and then, laboriously dragging in another, repeat the process.

An actor once said that he could always hear and see the breathing of one who played opposite him, if that one made a great point of breath control; that if he were to give advice to anyone along this line, he would tell him to relax the stomach. People grow tense if they are nervous, thus hindering natural expansion.

Right breathing will come easily if you will let that lift, that oomph which you hear in a gay folk song or popular tune, come into your outlook. Enjoy life, be grateful for it, and you will breathe deeply. Put all you have into the business of the moment, and you will breathe deeply. The deeper you think, the deeper you breathe.

Every English word contains open-throat sounds called vowels. As you learn to keep these sounds pure and unobstructed, all of your speech is improved.

It is more effective to practice the vowels standing than sitting. Take a good positive posture and have the tones come clear from your toes. Do not mind if someone hears you. Many a person has courage enough to practice singing for hours, causing the air to ring. Five or ten minutes of thoughtful exercise and experiment with these vowel sounds will bring immediate results in your voice.

Thinking of an open throat, breathe out through the mouth, then vocalize "I" forcefully, at the end of the breath. Again say the vowels: A...E...I...O...U..." One of these sounds is usually more free than the others. Which of yours sounds best to you? Give it between each of the other vowels. For example, if "O" were your best sound, say: "O..A..O..E..O..I..O..U.." If they still are not consistently good, again take the one which sounds best and join it as one sound to each of the other vowels: "O-A..O-E..O-I..O-OO.."

Place hands on hips. Say the whole alphabet in rhythm "A-B-C-D-E-F-G...H-I-J-K-L-M-N...O-P-Q-R-S-T-U....V-W-X-Y-Z...." You will feel a pressure against your hands as you give the letters. Simply let go in each pause.

Say explosively, *who, which, what.* Feel the expansion against your hands. Expand and try saying the whole alphabet on the one breath.

Say "Whoa!" as if you were pulling up four teams of horses. Repeat the vowels in the same tone feeling as if each sound comes from the soles of your feet. It is good for you to let out your voice in this way.

Say "Huh!" with the lips closed. Repeat it until you feel vibra-

tion when you place your fingers on each side of the bridge of
your nose. Again repeat the vowels.

Say *bl* before each vowel. "Blā. . .Blē. . .Blī. . .Blō. . .Blōō. . ."
The *bl* brings your words out on the lips and tip of the tongue
where they belong.

If you are inclined to let your voice settle down in your chest,
you can bring it forward where it belongs through seeing it
there. Say *A* in a repressed way. Now open your mouth and
push the *A* forward with the tongue. Say all of the vowels while
you have the voice placed correctly. Until this becomes natural
to you, frequently interrupt your reading aloud and bring the
voice forward with these exercises. One great contralto said that
in singing she thought of her words as being six inches in front
of her face. Doing this makes you feel that the voice is outside
the body and not that it is being forced out from the inside.
The moment the voice is forced, some of the power and
resonance is sacrificed.

I would say that a nasal tone is the most prevalent fault in
American speech. Because we hear it around us we unconsciously
adopt it. It is habitual, not natural, and usually has nothing to
do with the structure of the speech organs. It can be dropped.

There are only three sounds in our language which should
be wholly nasal—*m, n, ng*. When you hold your nose and say
the alphabet, all of the letters should be unchanged in sound
except the *m* and *n*. Feel the push on your fingers as you say
these two. If any of the others create this push, practice the
blā blē. . .exercise given in a preceding paragraph, followed by
the offending letters until they are out on the lips and tip of
the tongue.

The nasal tone is the result of a lazy soft palate, one which
does not shut off the nasal opening sufficiently, but allows sounds
other than the *m, n, ng* to go into the nasal cavity.

To define this fact for yourself, breathe through your nose
and say, *Ah*. Now yawn and repeat the sound. The nasal passage

is closed in the yawn, the tongue lies passively in the mouth and there is no trace of a nasal tone. Now say ă (the a in *and*). Notice how the front of the tongue is raised, pushing the sound forward. Repeat *and* several times. Practice the same way on *hand, sand, tan, man; aim, maim, name, plane; ounce, sound, mound, town.*

Words containing short ă as in *and,* long ā as in *aim, ow* as in *owl,* especially when the vowel is followed or preceded by *m, n,* or *ng,* are most likely to take on this nasal sound.

The time to correct mistakes in the voice is in practice, not when you are reading to others or speaking, for then you must be concerned only with the ideas you are giving out. To think of the way in which you read instead of the content of what you read will lead to affectation.

You are working for freedom in your voice, freedom from any physical tension and from temperamental tendencies. When you attain this freedom the voice becomes like a choice instrument tuned and ready to play.

In the vowel practice, one's shortcomings unexpectedly appear—uncertainty, hurry, fear, or dullness; a desire to force opinions on others, to be sweet, or intellectual; an undue sense of responsibility—I must, it's my duty; trying to please others; all such qualities show up in these simple sounds and have to be weeded out.

If you are not quite sure of yourself and are seeking the approval of the listeners, you are likely to give the vowels with a rising inflection. You will probably do the same thing when you talk, too. It is as if you were going to follow with, "Is this all right?" To remedy this attitude, think as you say each vowel, "Take it or leave it, here it is."

The hurrying type of person will not take time enough to think with each sound. He will rush from one vowel to the other without giving value to any. Should you belong to this group, make yourself silently count to five between each of the vowels.

You may find this almost impossible at first, but insist on doing it, and it will help to slow up your tempo in speaking as well.

If you talk in a small, negative tone, practice by pretending to make someone hear on the floor above you. Breathe deeply and have your whole body in the tone as you practice.

One who talks in a loud, flat tone, or in a dull one, needs inspiration. A new quality will appear in his voice if he will get a quiet listening sense before and as he practices.

One student who was practicing the vowels in a mechanical way was told to notice the shadows of the olive trees on the lawn, dark violet against the gold of late afternoon sun. She was then told to express what she saw, as she said the vowels. Immediately a colorful quality came into her tone; she had begun to think as she spoke instead of doing an exercise.

Another who came into class to improve a lifeless voice said that she had thought the proper way to be a secretary was to have a machinelike perfection of action. She had attempted to work in this fashion in her business and it naturally showed in a dull mechanical voice and a "dead pan" expression. After she began to see the value of inspiration and to use it in her office work, she said that she was far less tired at the end of the day than when she tried to work as a machine. Brightness came into her voice and face—the result of working in response to ideas instead of working with mechanical precision.

The one whose voice is inclined to soar excitedly should say the vowels at the floor. Make them positive and strong. A woman student, naturally lively and happy, objected to this remedy. "Why, it wouldn't be characteristic of me if I didn't have joy in my tones. Everyone always speaks about that in me." However, talking at the floor removed the effervescent quality from her voice without affecting its brightness.

Also do away with any circumflex or slide. A directing of the hand from the shoulder forward as you say each vowel, may help to keep your tone "straight from the shoulder."

One who speaks in a studied, "finished" manner, would do well to forget method and think rather of the spontaneity and naturalness of a child's speech. If one says the vowels simply and persists in this sort of practice, no useful technique will be lost. Only the superficial will drop away, the part that tends to make one self-conscious.

Thoughts of reserve, fear, suppression, criticism, and the like tighten the jaw. Should you be in the habit of setting your jaw and scarcely opening your mouth in talking, work to release it by stretching it open to the limit as you practice vowels. Even do it in front of a mirror, for you may think you are opening your mouth wide when you are not. While you may not overcome this tendency at once, thoughtful practice can get you to the place where you will not be restricted or controlled by these negatives as you speak.

All temperamental tendencies show in the tone. If you are able to recognize them, you can replace them with opposite qualities.

Harshness may appear from forcing oneself to go ahead when shyness urges one to retire, from selfishness, coarseness, or from heavy uninspired thinking. Visualize some of its antonyms in your vowel practice: ease, serenity, courtesy, gentleness, graciousness. Keeping an open throat is imperative in overcoming harshness in the voice.

Thin tones indicate that you are not valuing what you say. You need conviction of the importance of the idea and of your ability to express it.

Shallow tones indicate that you are not entirely in accord with what you are saying. Shyness, lack of confidence, self-depreciation, thinking about self, all contribute to causing a superficial tone. These negatives keep you from breathing deeply and from being wholeheartedly with your subject. Focus on the idea to the exclusion of all else, and you will have tones of depth and sincerity.

Those with muffled tones may be trying to cloak what they say, afraid to take a positive stand. Put it "on a candlestick" instead of "under a bushel." Honesty of thought, courage, clearness of vision, and a willingness to share what you see, are needed.

The whining tones of self-pity sound as if their owner feels that the world is against him, that he never gets any breaks. He is not thinking wholly of what he says, but is dwelling partly on himself. These tones can be corrected if this person learns to keep his "eye on the ball," on the idea which he is trying to express, and refuses to dwell on anything personal.

The sliding inflections associated with sweetness and a "peace-at-any-price" attitude are corrected by a "take-it-or-leave-it" thought which brings directness into the tone. You cannot be worried about whether you are pleasing everyone. You should seek to express ideas and let them stand or fall by their own virtue, refusing to take the responsibility for them.

He who booms out, bound that you shall hear and understand him, would quiet down if he would realize that the power is in the idea and not in himself. Listeners become suspicious when anything is forced on them in this egotistical way, and they mentally withdraw. Politicians, misled into this method, do not entice followers. Indeed, they harm their cause.

Men, when self-conscious, are inclined to talk down in their throats. This makes the words difficult to understand. The listener does not have an unclouded view and often will not make the effort to follow what is given in this inarticulate way. Let your voice be forthright and sure, as it is in your vowel practice, and people will enjoy listening to you.

Another habit, especially of men, is that of clearing the throat before starting to speak. This seems to say, "Now I have something to do. Ahem!" Swallowing is usually all that is necessary. Whispering the vowels with a little click in the back of the throat also helps to open it. One may do this without making an audible sound.

Recordings of your voice, which may be made in most music stores, help you to become conscious of your errors in diction, enunciation, and thought qualities. The public performer especially needs this check. You can detect your errors by carefully and impersonally listening to the recordings. If there is wrong thought quality in the voice, refer again to this chapter, which analyzes many general mistakes. Should your difficulty not be mentioned, look up the word which exemplifies it in *Roget's Thesaurus* or some other book of synonyms and antonyms. Study the antonyms which give you the corrective. If you can see that your voice needs to be more positive, or more clear, or warmer, you can remedy your difficulty. You can prove to yourself that thought brings a change in the tone. Experiment as you practice the vowels by mentally replacing any unpleasant tendency with its opposite quality.

Volume is dependent on the speaker's ability to visualize. Off on a camping trip when you want to speak to someone, you pitch your voice without premeditation and reach him if he is within earshot. So volume should always be regulated—by recognizing those who are interested in hearing what you say or read, and by knowing that the idea you are expressing includes making this particular group hear and understand what you give. Sensing the hearer should take care of the technical side of your speech, just as it does when you are outdoors and unconscious of method. There is no need to throw or "project the voice to the last seat." Feel rather that you include those in the last seat. They are a part of the idea you are expressing. José Iturbi said, when asked how he made people in the galleries of large halls hear the most delicate tones, "I intend them to hear." You can take care of voice volume in the same way—by intention.

For practice in this, put your hands on your sides below the waist. Say the vowels, mentally including the room in which you are practicing. Now visualize a place the size of a small hall and say them. Seeing a large auditorium with which you are familiar, considering the balconies and the seats under them, say the vowels again. Do not force; only visualize. When you think of the auditorium you will doubtless feel more expansion in your body and you will speak more slowly than you do when you try to fill the small room. These adjustments come about spontaneously as you are free from self-consciousness.

In addressing a large group, no attempt should be made to spread the voice over the whole auditorium or it will sound thin and vague. Focus your speech, as if speaking to one person, then your message sounds direct and intimate to everyone. However, this does not mean to pick out one individual in the auditorium and address him alone. The listeners are all one in receptivity to the idea, and it is this oneness which you address regardless of which individual your eyes happen to rest upon.

At first you may have to think consciously of the technical points covered in this chapter. It has been said that we have to go through four stages in learning any technique. First, *unconscious incompetency*, i.e., we do not know we are talking with a closed throat. Second, *conscious incompetency*—we hear a recording of our voice and realize that something is wrong. We must do something about it. Third, *conscious competency*—we read this chapter and practice the points suggested here. Fourth, *unconscious competency* (a happy state)—as open throat becomes natural to us.

As simple as these few suggestions are, if followed they will produce almost immediate results. A free, expressive voice is everyone's natural heritage.

Chapter *13*

PRESERVE THE BEAUTY
OF THE ENGLISH LANGUAGE

"The English language fell from his tongue with that candid simplicity which is its genius and with that grandeur which is its glory," said Dorothy Thompson, speaking of Sir Winston Churchill.

English has adopted illustrative words from many tongues; consequently it can express shades of feeling, color, form, materials, situations, qualities of thought, ideas, and metaphysical truths which cannot always be conveyed in other languages. Appreciation and understanding of the beauty and richness of English stimulate the desire to bring out its potentialities in speech, and to protect it from the corruptions of dialects and slovenly usage. At the same time there is no condemnation of the use of expressive and pithy slang, which keeps a language alive.

The natural beauty of English is apparent when it is spoken with an open throat and with clear, pure vowel sounds. Its rhythm appears in a lengthening of these sounds in the accented syllables and a shortening of the vowels in the unaccented syllables.

Meaning is visualized through the vowel sounds. Their importance to the English language can scarcely be exaggerated. A singing teacher once said that, when singing, vowels should be like the width of the room, consonants like the wallpaper. In a lesser degree, this should also be true in speaking.

The consonants give individuality to the vowel sounds, forming them into words. Consonants should be clear-cut and short but not explosive. It takes an alive thought to give consonants the right enunciation. Some localities are marked by slovenly speech because people slur over their consonants or drop them altogether, as *Le' me cu min,* for *Let me come in; a'je'tiv* for *adjective; reco'nize* for *recognize.* On the other hand the pedantic or overconscientious often make final consonants sound as if a vowel occurred after them: *rib* becomes *rib-ba; God, Godda; egg, egg-ga; live, liv-va.* They will also end final *f, k, p, t,* with an audible puff of air. One should come up to these consonants and stop with nicety.

Many people are unconscious that they neglect certain consonants. It is slovenly speech to pronounce *acts—ax, facts—fax, gifts—gifs, exists—exis-s-s.* To overcome this laziness, do a little experimenting (not expirimenting). Make the *t*-sound. Notice that you give a puff of air at the end of the sound. Now say *act.* You end it with the puff of air. Repeat the word but stop as you come to the *t*-sound, tongue against the upper gums, and hold it there a moment. You know you have the *t* in the word now. Then a tiny slide of the tongue causes the *s* sound. A little practice will enable you to make the *s* very short. The reason the *t* is often omitted is because the tongue is lazy. It takes an alert movement to bring the tip up to the *t.* As a result many are satisfied to allow *hosts* to be *hos-s-s.* To practice on the *sts* sound, make a prolonged *s* sound, really a hiss, and interrupt it with the *t:* s-s-s-t-s-s-t-s-s-t-s. Now practice on *exists, hosts, fists, posts.*

Do not let the word *actually,* which is pronounced AK choo uh ly, become AK sh̲oo uhly. Do not let *lecture,* which is pronounced LEK ch (er), become LEK sh̲ (er).

To correct a habit of saying *goin'* for *going,* sound *n* alone; notice where the tongue is placed, on upper gums. Now sound *ng* and see how differently you use your tongue. It is simple to overcome "dropping final g's" as the habit is incorrectly called. The difficulty really lies in using a wrong consonant sound, not in dropping the *g.*

Review Chapters 9 and 10 in order to learn the proper way to shorten unaccented syllables and words. It is extremely important to incorporate this knowledge into your reading and speaking.

Exaggerated lip movement, such as the French use in their language, is not characteristic of English.

Some phoneticians, especially those who like to delve into dialects and their history, and into the evolution of our tongue, resent any interference with the vernacular used in each community. This is unfortunate. I attended a university class in phonetics and American pronunciation, filled with young people who wanted to improve their speech. The professor implied that it would lead to affectation if they tried to change their pronunciation. He entirely ignored the fact that a distinct dialect, besides corrupting the language, is detrimental to the individual using it. When people notice how you say a thing they cannot give full attention to what you say. If you would have people understand your speech, be as free as possible from mannerisms in pronunciation—such as a Southern drawl, the nasal twang of New England, the peculiarities of the Middle West, and West, and foreign inflections.

Many Americans, when it is suggested to them that they alter their diction, exclaim, "Not me! I'd sound affected if I changed my way of speaking." If anything is correct it is not affected. The fact that you were not born in a section of the country where beautiful speech is used should not condemn you to the use of an unpleasant dialect for a whole lifetime. It is possible to correct any wrong diction and still keep your naturalness. *If you see the thought expressed by a word as you say it, you will not sound affected.* It is only when you think of *how* you say a word that you sound unnatural.

There are three steps in correcting yourself. First, awaken to your mistakes. Second, find good, accepted forms to replace the incorrect or unpleasant ones you have been using. Third, make the newly found forms your own through repeating them many times.

If you are accustomed to hearing and using wrong forms, you may not know that you are doing it. Listening—to yourself and others—makes you aware of your errors. This book cannot attempt to give corrections for the many dialects, but can take up only the most noticeable errors in general American diction.

To find good accepted forms familiarize yourself with a good standard dictionary. Study its key. Study its foreword. Take time to master it so that you can use it with authority.

Many words have more than one correct pronunciation. We have at present no style of English which is accepted as correct in all parts of the world, although the International Phonetic Association is attempting to establish such a one. However, television, motion pictures and radio, the speed of communication and transportation, our common causes and shared interests, are bringing all English-speaking peoples in closer touch with one another, and as an inevitable result, the differences in pronunciation are lessening. Until there is an internationally accepted form, the best we can do in improving our speech is to choose one that is not conspicuous in our locality, one that visualizes the idea for which it stands, is euphonious, and is considered correct.

Fear of what others think should not influence your selection.

Pope's advice about choice of words is just as good with regard to pronunciation:

> In words, as fashions, the same rule will hold;
> Alike fantastic if too new or old.
> Be not the first by whom the new is tried,
> Nor yet the last to lay the old aside.

I feel about pronunciation a good deal as Henry Ward Beecher felt about grammar. When a zealot pointed out grammatical errors in his sermon, he said, "Young man, when the English language gets in my way, it doesn't stand a chance."

In looking up doubtful words in the dictionary, be sure that you understand the key to pronunciation. Know you are correct before you attempt to change.

Lastly and most important, *repeat the correction many times.* Repeat and repeat. You can do this at off times—as you drive, or work in the garden. Then your ear and speech organs get used to the feel of the right form. Speech, being mechanical, has to be corrected by the mechanical procedure of constant repetition. It is practicing the right form, not merely finding it, which makes a correction permanent.

The first sign of improvement is that you become conscious when you use the wrong form. It will torment you, but cheer up! You are well on the road to recovery when you become aware of mistakes. A few more good pushes and you will be over the top. Soon the proper form will automatically come to the lips.

To correct yourself at the time of reading or speaking before others, makes you sound affected, because your thought has shifted from the subject matter to the way in which you are expressing it. "Never practice tennis strokes in a tournament," William Tilden said. By the same rule, correcting diction should be a separate process from reading and speaking.

Focus on one sound at a time. Trying to correct many sounds at once is discouraging. One sound learned, will perfect a group of similar words. When you notice that the final syllable of *yellow* is ō not *uh* you will correct your pronunciation of *window, follow, piano,* et cetera. You can then forget this group and go on to another sound.

This kind of practice does not take long. It calls rather for intelligent use of the time spent. Before starting, give your voice a workout with the vowels and follow this with the pronunciations you are correcting. While you are working to better your diction, reading aloud should be done at least daily. During this reading, if your voice tires or does not sound clear, say a few vowels to ensure an open throat, the whole of you in the tone, and the words out on your lips.

The sound of the vowel *a* varies according to its position in the mouth. *Ā-ale* is the most forward. *Ă-am* is back slightly; then *ȧ-ask, ä-art, ạ-all*. Take the sounds alone, *ạ, ä, ȧ, ă, ā,* and you will feel them come forward. Consider the *a* which Webster marks with one dot above it (ȧ), the *a* in *ask*. This is approximately the sound of "Ah" said with slightly smiling lips. It is not the broad *ä-art* produced when the jaw is dropped. Say the short *ă* as in *am*. Then relax or drop the tongue slightly and you will give this sound correctly. Or another way to place this sound is to say *ä* as in *art,* and then bring it forward. When you get the sound, use it in the word *ask*. Take different words which have this sound and repeat each until it feels natural: *last, pass, class, path, rather, glass, can't*.

Much opposition to this particular sound is raised by those who love naturalness, because it is usually the first speech correction attempted by those who are "trying to be elegant." This group will even use *ah* for the short *a* (ă), saying "Ahnd I saw a hahppy mahn. . ." There is no justification for this pronunciation. It is entirely incorrect.

Most people do not object to hearing a short *a* (ă) sound in place of the one dot *ȧ,* because it is in such general usage throughout the United States. However, *ȧ* is in good taste in any part of the English-speaking world, but there are locations where the *ă* used in place of the *ȧ* is considered a crudity.

To avoid the nasal sound with the short *ă,* open the throat by saying the vowels and practice these words: *ănd, sănd, mănn, tăn, hăppy, căn, hăve, hăd, ăm, Phărisee*. If you still have difficulty in keeping them free from a nasal twang say Tă-, tă-, tă-, tăn. Hă-, hă-, hă-, hănd. Mă-, mă, mă-, măn.

To avoid sounding affected employ these two rules:

1. Visualize the meaning of the words as you practice.
2. Lean on the vowels; do not pronounce them gingerly.

When you make these improvements in your speech, family or close friends often object, preferring to keep you in the little pigeonhole where they have placed you. Notwithstanding, they will like the improvement, if you dare to continue until you reach "unconscious competency."

The fact that you are not always consistent in the process of correcting pronunciation need not bother you. Persons who from birth have used these sounds do not always say them the same.

Work on *a*'s for several days. Look up common words containing *a* if you are not sure of their sound, and add them to your lists. Not until you feel satisfied that you have made headway with them, should you take up another incorrect sound.

If you are from the Middle West or the West in the United States, with the exception of San Francisco, you probably grind your *r*'s. This sound makes speech harsh and ugly. A theatrical pronunciation, one that uses an emphasized *ah* in place of r, (*fi-ah'* for *fire*) is not advised; only a softening of *r* when it has a *semi-vowel character,* that is, *when it comes after a vowel sound and before a consonant.* R is not regarded as a consonant in this position but serves merely to alter and lengthen the vowel sound. Examples of this are *heart, Lord, park, part.* It is customary in the West almost to lose the vowel sound in these words. *Heart* becomes *hr-r-rt.* Without a vowel sound the beauty of the word is lost. Try saying the word, thinking only of the vowel. Say, "Ha-a-a-rt." Barely touch the *r* as you say the *t.* If you keep the word forward in the mouth, you will not grind the *r.* Notice that the tip of the tongue is back of the lower teeth as you say the vowels. Practice keeping it in this position when saying this semi-vowel *r* in *ark, church, earth, Lord.*

Get *r*-conscious for a while. Listen to speakers on television and observe how they handle *r*'s. The more you listen, the more clearly you will see that the *r* mars the beauty of speech when it is always used as a consonant.

Final *r*'s also should be obscured. Final unaccented *-er, -or, -yr, -ar* should sound much as the final syllable of *sofa*. They should be inconspicuous and at a lower level than the accented syllable. Say the following words, making the accented syllables positive and shortening the last syllables to this neutral vowel sound: <u>fath</u>(er), <u>broth</u>(er), cre<u>at</u>(or), <u>read</u>(er), <u>li</u>(ar), <u>zeph</u>(yr). Listen for this sound in the speech of others until you get the model you prefer, then practice it. It may help to imitate some-one who uses *r*'s correctly. Say to yourself, "John always says 'fath-a' instead of fath<u>er</u>." Then, while you have the model, repeat it many times.

Almost the same mistake can be made with the *l* as with the *r*. When the *l* is pronounced with the tongue curled back, it is an awkward sound. As the *l* is brought forward, back of the upper front teeth, it has beauty. Say *flesh* with the tongue curled back. Now try it with the tongue forward in the mouth and the *l* delicate. Say *people*. Again keep the *l* forward in the mouth and as short as possible. Do not let it be heavy as if it had a vowel sound before it, *peo-pul*.

Wide variety exists in the pronunciation of long *u* in both accented and unaccented syllables. It varies from *y-ōō, ĭ-ōō*, to *ōō*. Although many condemn as incorrect the use of this *ōō* sound in words marked long *u*, still most of the leading authori-ties admit that many educated speakers, especially in America, use these pronunciations (dōōty for dūty). Nevertheless, the diphthong sound, *ĭ-ōō* or *y-ōō*, is preferred for the long *u* sound.

Words beginning with *u* are always given the *y-ōō* sound, as *unite* (*y-ōō-nĭt*).

It is also easy and customary to give the long *u* in words when *u* occurs after *b* (*beauty*), after *c* (*cube*), *f* (*few*), *g* (*gew gaw*), *h* (*human*), *k* (*Kew*), *m* (*mute*), *p* (*pure*).*

* Words taken from *Webster's New International Dictionary, Second Edition.*

The words where the variation occurs, where the long *u* is given an $\overline{oo}$ sound by many, are words where *u* occurs after *s* (*assume*), *z* (*resume*), *th* (*enthusiast*), *d* (*duty*), *t* (*tune*), *n* (*new*).

After *l* good usage is divided, both forms being used (*Lūke* and *Lōōk*).

After *l* and another consonant in the same syllable, $\overline{oo}$ is used as in *blue* (*blōō*), *include* (*inclōōd*).

After *r*, $\overline{oo}$ is used as in *true*, *rule*.

The long sound of *u* should be used inconspicuously. A little practice will help you to do this without sounding overprecise. Again make lists of these words for practice. After looking them up in a dictionary, repeat them until they feel natural to you.

Another common mistake is the pronunciation of *wh* as if it were *w* alone. *Wheat* is miscalled *weet; white, wite*. *Wh* should be pronounced as if it were *hw*, or a voiceless *w*. There is little difference between the two. *Went* starts with a voiced *w*. *Where* starts with a voiceless *w*, made by blowing air through lips shaped for the *w* sound.

For fuller study of these and other phonetic sounds, consult a good dictionary or book on phonetics. This chapter can only awaken you to some of the most common mistakes. A great help in improving diction is observation. Through it you become conscious of that which is beautiful in pronunciation. As you form models in thought, you can bring them into your speech by the method described above: thoughtful repetition of them until they feel natural to you and become your own.

By the same method you can add to your vocabulary. When you hear a particularly apt word or phrase, determine its pronunciation and exact meaning. Then repeat it many times. Put it into sentences and repeat them. Stay with it until it feels natural to you. Soon you will use it with authority. Reading good literature brings new words and phrases into your conversation.

A German philologist says of the English language: "It has a thorough power of expression, such as no other language ever possessed. It may truly be called a world-language, for no other can compare with it in richness, reasonableness, and solidity of texture."

A British poet has presented the special features of the European languages in the following poem:

> Greek's a harp we love to hear;
> Latin is a trumpet clear;
> Spanish like an organ swells;
> Italian rings its bridal bells;
> France with many a frolic mien,
> Tunes her sprightly violin;
> Loud the German rolls his drum
> When Russia's clashing cymbals come;
> But British sons may well rejoice,
> For English is the human voice.
>
> —JOSEPH WILD, D.D., "The Lost Ten Tribes"

Let us respect this language and preserve its beauty and purity in our speech.

Chapter *14*

THE FINE ART OF
READING ALOUD

This chapter is not for the casual reader. Without thoughtful experimentation and analysis it may prove confusing, but it is indispensable to the one who wishes to perfect his reading ability. It also has significant points for anyone who interprets —whether it be the interpretation of nature into a picture, the interpretation of a piece of music into a piano solo, or the interpretation of a character in a play into a performance. The focus, however, is on the interpretation of written words into reading aloud.

Pure or impersonal reading is reading which brings the subject into view wholly by the use of the reader's visualizing power and ability to express what he sees in words. It is free of gesture, action, and impersonation, although the mood and characteristics of a person may be suggested in the manner of reading direct discourse. This reading can come closer to reality than can acting, because in reading the scene of the drama takes place in the thought of the listener and knows no limit of time, space, or locality. In the theater you are given the director's concept of the play which may or may not coincide with what the author saw when he wrote it. But in pure reading, the listener is given the ideas themselves and left free to see them as he will.

This type of reading demands listening keen enough to penetrate to the ideas behind the words. Then there must be a warm response to them, identification with them, until the reading becomes a spontaneous expression of what the reader sees and feels. In fact, good reading is a resurrection—the dead words open out into living ideas. Think how we may take a book down from the shelf—one that looks dusty, aged, dull— and through reading aloud, give others a picture of events which happened two thousand years ago, enable them to see the people of that time, their environment, sense their thinking, feel their very presence, arrive at the same state of mind as the author's at the time he wrote the book.

If reading is to attain this height, it must shake itself loose from the limitations of personal interpretation and move along with the power and beauty of the idea itself. Then, as you listen to it, you are not conscious that a person is reading because the ideas come directly to your thought in all their color, life, and vividness, free from any mannerisms or artificial emphasis by the reader. This reading is as impersonal as a trial balance, simple as a child's reply, yet it is warm and vigorous.

But the dullest, most colorless, most lifeless reading is heard under the guise of impersonal reading. No matter how much a reader has previously grasped of the subject matter, if he is not impressed by it at the instant he reads, his reading is dead letter.

St. Paul in the fourteenth chapter of First Corinthians condemned speech that had intellectuality but no inspiration. He said of it, "For thou verily givest thanks well, but the other is not edified." Even though the words are correctly spoken, if reading is lifeless and heavy through the vain attempt to make it impersonal, if it is trained and self-conscious because the reader's thought is filled with technique, or if it merely does not visualize because of a half-asleep mentality, the listener "is not edified." The purpose of reading is thwarted.

Pure reading has certain techniques which can be learned through thoughtful practice. It requires:

1. Timing—that is, listening through each illustrative word for its meaning just as you say it.
2. Laws of Conversational Reading—which help you to bring out the full meaning.
3. Conversational Pronunciation—which gives your reading the rhythm of speaking.
4. Highlights and Perspective—which come inspirationally to the one who listens and visualizes as he reads, but must be recognized and preserved in order to ensure perfect performance.

Timing

A great deal has already been written in this book about timing in speech. It has been given as the most important law of reading. To satisfy yourself about this importance read the following verses in a monotone but with right timing, that is, with your thought on the meaning of the word just as you say it.

Therefore will not we fear, though the earth be removed, and though the mountains be carried into the midst of the sea; though the waters thereof roar and be troubled, though the mountains shake with the swelling thereof.

PSALM 46:2, 3

If you really keep your timing, the meaning will appear in spite of the monotone. These same verses are transcribed later under *Highlights and Perspective,* in order to illustrate how visualizing will bring natural highlights into the reading.

Laws of Conversational Reading

Good readers comply with these laws unconsciously. Many of them are found in Chapter 11 and in this chapter. They will help you to grasp and give out the full meaning of what you read.

Conversational Pronunciation

Reading is like wood carving. It is what you cut away that brings out the pattern. Thus, slighting unimportant or repetitious words helps to bring the illustrative words into bold relief. Study Chapters 9 and 10 for instruction on accepted methods of slighting unaccented words and syllables.

Highlights and Perspective

Reread the above selection from Psalm 46 and allow the highlights to appear. Then consult the following transcription:

Therefore will not we fear. . . , though the earth (be) removed, (and though the) mountains (be) carried (into the) midst (of the) sea; (though the waters) thereof roar (and be) troubled, (though the mountains) shake (with the) swelling (thereof).*

From this transcription you will notice the way highlights appear in reading:

a. Through use of the pause. This is shown after the word *fear* which establishes the theme—to *not fear,* no matter what happens. Without this pause the listener will rarely grasp this point clearly.
b. By lengthening the vowel, as in *roar.*
c. By a higher pitch, as in the word *sea.*
d. By greater intensity, as in the word *shake.*

Perspective appears in the reading as words and phrases take different places on the stage of thought, like characters in a play. Some should be highlighted, others subordinated. I beg of you that you do not try to figure this out with the intellect. This is the cause of most of the stilted, uninteresting reading which we hear. The way to capture this perspec-

* H over a word means read it with a higher pitch. Key to Transcriptions on pp. 235-37.

tive is to read with a listening ear and let inspiration show
you the underlying theme of the passage and the relative importance of the words. Expect these to appear with the first
reading, but if your listening is not yet keen enough, or if you
do not thoroughly understand the meaning of all the words,
stay with what you are reading until it is clarified in your
thought. Should you be reading the Bible, it is often helpful
to go to the Hebrew and Greek vocabularies in the back of
Strong's *Exhaustive Concordance of the Bible* and get the
original meaning and derivation of the word in question, as
well as finding the definition, synonyms, and antonyms from
English dictionaries. This research is like the craftsman's
sharpening of his tools. With this fuller understanding of the
words again think, "What do these words say?" and listen as
you reread. The penetrating quality of listening opens out the
most obscure passage.

You will doubtless notice that you read the less important
thoughts at a quicker tempo, or with less intensity, or sometimes at a lower level. When you read a certain passage in an
inspired way, if you will have some method of marking the
passage, you will not lose the pattern even when you are before
a group. Learn how to hold what inspiration tells you, and you
can be sure of consistently good reading.

Words which are subordinate should not be hurried over with
a *studied* technique. This brings an artificial flavor to the reading. When you read rapidly you must still visualize. Never
say words without thought. Remember that the thought is to
the reader what paint is to the artist.

For practice in perspective read the following excerpt from
the story of the Good Samaritan. A man has been wounded by
thieves and left by the roadside, half dead.

> And by chance there came down a certain priest that
> way: and when he saw him, he passed by on the other side.

And likewise a Levite, when he was at the place, came and looked on him, and passed by on the other side. But a certain Samaritan, as he journeyed, came where he was: and when he saw him, he had compassion on him, and went to him, and bound up his wounds, pouring in oil and wine, and set him on his own beast, and brought him to an inn, and took care of him.—LUKE 10:31-34

In the following transcription some phrases are less conspicuous because they repeat an idea already in the picture. These are placed in parentheses. Others need to be slighted because they are not particularly vital to the story. I have placed an "L" at the beginning of these phrases to indicate that they should come in at a lower level, and have also looped the phrase to the one following so that only a slight pause will be given here. A perceptible pause, you remember, gives value to a thought. Of course the "L" used before some members of the series of things which the Samaritan did, is not to indicate a phrase of less importance, but to show the natural variance of tone in the different members of a series. The variation is slight but essential. Every phrase has its own tempo, pitch, quality.

With the exception of the first word, the many *and*'s are completely obscured. They become a mere vocal pulse at a low pitch, not a spoken word. Experiment with yourself on this by looking away from the page and giving the words as if you were telling someone of the incident. This carving out of the unstressed words is most important to your artistry in reading.

And ⌊(by chance) there came down a certain priest that way: and when he saw him . . . , he passed by on the other side.

(And likewise a) Levite, ⸀(when he was at the place), came and looked (on him), ⌊(and passed by on the other side). (But a certain) Samaritan, ⌊as he journeyed, (came where he was): and when he (saw him), (he had) compassion (on him), ⌊and went to him, and bound up his wounds, pouring in oil (and) wine, ⌊and set him on his own beast, and <u>brought</u> him (to an) inn, ⌐and took care of him.

I have heard readers make a great point of the reading of the phrase "came where he was." When I have questioned why, they have said that this was the wonderful thing, that the Samaritan *came where he was.* They take the phrase out of the context and use it to illustrate meeting a person in need right where he is. I agree that that is a good point, and that we have a right to learn all we can from the Bible narratives. But in pure reading we cannot twist the words to mean other than they were intended to mean in their present context. Each of the travelers had come where the man was. As you continue reading you will see that the Samaritan has not yet seen the man. The next phrase says, "and when he saw him." We must be as pure in our reading as Toscanini is in his musical interpretation— we must let the words tell what they will.

Reading is not impersonal when the reader thunders it out at you, or when he runs along on the surface, or when he hits certain words, bound to make you see what he wants you to see. Such a reader read Ecclesiastes 2 in this way:

Incorrect: I made <u>me</u> great work; I builded <u>me</u> houses; I planted <u>me</u> vineyards: I made <u>me</u> gardens and orchards, and I planted trees. . . .

He, of course, wanted to impress the listener with the fact that Solomon did everything for himself. However, this was not what the printed words said. They said:

Correct: I made me great work;⌐(I builded me) <u>houses</u>; (I planted me) vineyards . . . : Then I looked (on all the works that my hands had wrought, and on the labour that I had laboured to do); and . . . , behold . . , all (was) vanity and vexation of <u>spirit,</u>ʌ(and there was no) <u>profit</u> under the sun. [Read "under the sun" as a superlative, as if you were saying "anywhere on earth."]

This last rendering brings out the point in an impersonal way. It lets you visualize all of the efforts made by Solomon to gain satisfaction. Then it brings you to a conclusion which teaches its lesson with strength and conviction. The incorrect transcription stated in the first three words, "I made *me*," that this is going to teach you what happens if you are self-centered. The listener is apt to rebel at this too apparent moralizing. But in the second reading a picture is painted which tells its own tale, undimmed by any preaching.

In explaining this point of impersonal expression, a New York singing teacher told a student that the saying, "All the world loves a lover," was not true. All the world makes fun of a lover if he is caught showing his affection. But all the world loves a song that gives each listener the experience of being a lover or loved. The singer was told to sing a love song so that the listeners would not think that the experience happened to the singer, but to themselves. So must we read, not rehearsing a personal experience but visualizing ideas so vividly that they become each listener's personal experience. When reading the 23rd Psalm, we should not cause the listener to feel that God is *our* shepherd, by saying "the Lord is my shepherd," but instead should see the meaning of *shepherd* so clearly that each listener would feel he was cared for.

The same point was made by a currently successful actor who said that it was the purpose of the actor to inspire, or pass on emotions, not to live them himself; that he let the audience do the suffering. As in the theater, the reader must see and bring the idea to light impersonally, letting the audience do the emotional reacting. He must go against the emotional mood.

Gide wrote that a reader should be "but a brute utterly unaware of the pathos of the scene he is describing, and that the tragic element comes from the very fact that he doesn't know that what he is telling is tragic; he ought to go in the contrary direction to his story. . . . The listener will be all the more moved the less he (the reader) is himself. . . ." While I would not describe as radically as has Gide, the restraint of emotion which is necessary on the part of the reader, still we do need to keep this ideal firmly in mind: *When you read, report— don't give opinions or personal reactions.*

If the reader is self-indulgent and roars with laughter during the reading of a humorous anecdote, the listeners may be amused at the laughter but probably will not get the point of the story. The best comedian tells the story graphically and leaves the laughter for the audience.

Should the reader shed tears in a sad passage, it embarrasses the listener and turns him from the ideas to a person. But if the reader refuses to think about himself and his own feelings, he has done his part: that of seeing the ideas which the author saw when he wrote, and portraying them so that all who hear will seem to have the actual experience.

When reading a sad passage, such as the description of Jesus' last supper with his disciples, there should still be light and life in the reading. The reader would dull the picture if he gave in to the mood. He must keep the picture in clear colors no matter what the mood. To read this passage in a dead voice or in a melancholy circumflex would be equivalent to using muddy colors if you were painting it. Remember the brilliancy of color in Leonardo da Vinci's "Last Supper."

The artist needs to drop all of his personal feelings and be at the service of the idea. He must be the seeing of the idea, not the emotional reacting to the seeing of this idea. Again let me repeat: he must report, not give opinions.

The reader always reads *with* his audience, not *to* it. Before he starts he should listen—that is, quiet self-consciousness and turn undistracted attention to the printed page. Then as he reads aloud, his listening takes him through the words to the very ideas which inspired the author to write. The ideas are given a new body, a new expression, by means of the voice and visualizing power of the reader. This is the resurrection, the ideas brought to life—for the reader, by means of going through the printed words; for the auditors, by going through the spoken words. Both the reader and audience are listening to the same ideas coming to them through different mediums of expression.

To the reader as well as to the listeners the meaning must be unfolding as if for the first time. Although he is reading aloud, his attitude should never be: I know what this means and I'm telling you. He recognizes the listeners before he starts. He observes the number who are present. If he is at ease, this appraisal automatically takes care of the volume of his voice. Then he centers his whole attention on listening to the meaning of what he reads.

With this method he will never *read down* in the tone a kindergarten teacher uses for the "dear children"; never will he read in an apologetic tone; never patronizingly; never with condemnation; never "sweetly"; never without interest.

If he lets himself think of the sacredness of the Bible as he reads it, his tone will be hushed and perhaps he will chant the words. The listener knows that the reader respects the Bible, but that is not the reader's function. Let him tell what the Bible says, then the listener decides for himself about its merit.

The reader may be double-minded and fear his auditors will think he is condemning them. This brings an apologetic circumflex into the reading. His tone will say, "I'm-sorry-to-have-to-say-this-but-" while his words are, "Ye are of your father the devil." Or he may feel that the people ought to know these facts, and begin to preach at them. The listeners, being sensitive, will resent this quality and quietly pull down the curtain of their thought and stop listening. He tells them, "Ye are of your father the devil," in a condemning tone. This is personal and thoroughly objectionable to most people.

But with an honest approach, letting the words unfold to him and uttering them as if he were thinking them *to himself,* the reading will become strong, positive, and impersonal. He is addressing a quality of thinking, not an individual, and he enjoys saying to it, "Ye are of your father the devil."

Law underlies the interpretation of English words placed in a certain order. Expression should not be a matter of what you think or of what someone else thinks, but of what the words say. Seldom is there similarity in the reading of the same passage, but this is because so few people understand impersonal interpretation. Unable to lose their self-consciousness, or not aware of the full significance of the words they read, they give only an approximation of the meaning.

Nazimova said that sometimes she did not thoroughly see the pattern of her role in a play until four or five weeks after the opening. Up to that time she had not reached the full essence of the part. But once the pattern was attained, she stayed with it in every performance. This did not mean that subsequent performances were imitations of previous ones, but that each time she went back to the underlying idea, felt its inspiration and motivating power, and this empathy with the idea inevitably produced the right pattern.

Readers also have this experience. I have heard accomplished readers from different parts of the country, with dissimilar training but with a knowledge of the science of reading, give the same selection with scarcely any variation.

People immediately think: "Well, in that case, would not all reading sound alike?"

You do not have to worry about this happening. When anything is read exactly right the listener will probably not even know that it has been read to him. He will seem to have thought or experienced the ideas and not merely heard them. It is your mannerisms, your temperamental tendencies, which cause diversity in the reading of the same passage. When these are out of the way, you are free to portray an infinite variety of qualities, whether it be the poetry of a David, the despair of a Judas, the wonder of a Mary, or the impetuosity of a Peter.

Be awake to mood when you read. Your consciousness of it will bring the technique needed for its expression—that is, alter the quality of your tone, change the tempo, the tone pattern, the emphasis. Every selection has its own inner rhythm, a rhythm of sound and pause, but these are nothing without the thought of the reader to give meaning. Through good listening you will feel when the mood of a selection changes. Mark, in some way, the places where this change occurs. I use *Ch* to indicate a change of mood.

The 93rd Psalm has two such changes in it. It would be helpful to you if you would turn to it and read it first from the Bible, expecting the meaning to unfold with the first reading. Then compare the way you read it with the way it is marked here.

The Lord reigneth, he is clothed with majesty; (the Lord is clothed with) <u>strength</u>, wherewith (he hath) girded himself .... : the world also (is established), (that it) <u>cannot</u> (be) <u>moved</u>. . . . Thy throne (is established) <u>of old</u>: (thou art from) <u>everlasting</u>. . . . . [Change, as if you said, "On the other hand."] The <u>floods</u> have <u>lifted up</u>, ∟(O Lord), (the floods have lifted up their) <u>voice</u>; F (the floods lift up their) waves. . . . . [Change again to first mood, as with a full organ and low pitch.] The Lord on high is mightier than the noise of <u>many</u> waters, <u>yea</u>, F than the mighty waves of the <u>sea</u> . . . Thy testimonies are very <u>sure</u>: <u>holiness</u> becometh thine house, ∟(O Lord), for <u>ever</u>.

In pure reading the meaning alone determines the way you read, except when you are reading direct discourse. Even here you do not attempt to impersonate the voice of the speaker, as an actor does, but a penetrating discernment of his mood and character will cause them to show subtly in your tone, emphasis, and tempo. When I discover the mood of the speaker, I often indicate it in the margin. For example in the fourth Chapter of John is the story of Jesus' meeting with the woman of Samaria. He asked her for a drink.

curious
coy

Then saith the woman of Samaria unto him, how is it that thou, being a Jew, askest drink of me, which am a woman of Samaria? for the Jews have no dealings with the Samaritans.

man speaking impersonal

Jesus answered and said unto her, If thou knewest the gift of God, and who it is that saith to thee, Give me to drink; thou wouldest have asked of him, and he would have given thee living water.

surprise

The woman saith unto him, Sir, thou hast nothing to draw with, and the well is deep: from whence then hast thou that living water?

When the woman found that he was a prophet, because he had been able to tell her that she had "had five husbands; and he whom thou now hast is not thy husband. . . ." she began to ask him thoughtful questions about worshiping God, which Jesus answered, ending with:

man speaking

God (is a) Spirit: and they that worship him must worship (him in spirit) and in truth.

This note, man speaking, is to help the reader avoid the saccharine tones often used for this verse. It should be straight from the shoulder in character.

A woman usually has much more circumflex and change of pitch in her speaking than a man does—the more effusive she is, the more slides in her voice. A patronizing, placating, apologetic, or self-justifying person also uses circumflex in his tones.

When Jesus had healed a man through casting out a devil, it is related of the multitude, Luke 4:36, 37:

> And they were all amazed. . ., and spake among them-
> selves, saying. . ., [wonder] <u>What</u> a <u>word</u> is this! (for
> with) authority (and) power he commandeth the <u>unclean</u>
> <u>spirits</u>, and they <u>come</u> <u>out</u>. . . . . [change to **nar**] and the
> fame of him went out into every place of the <u>country</u> round
> about.

The first part of this discourse is simple narrative. Then in
the direct discourse you feel the mood of wonderment. Then
the tone changes again to narrative.

When a proclamation is being made, as in Daniel 3:4-6,
you would not intone it loudly in pure reading as you would if
you were giving it on the stage. Still you would not use the same
tone as you use in simple narrative.

> Therefore, an herald cried aloud. . ., [proclaim] To you it
> is commanded, O people, nations, and languages, that at
> what time ye hear the sound of the cornet, flute, harp,
> sackbut, psaltery, dulcimer, and all kinds of musick, ye
> fall down and worship the golden image that Nebuchad-
> nezzar the king hath set up: and whoso falleth <u>not</u> down
> and worshippeth shall the same hour be cast into the midst
> of a burning fiery furnace. . . .**nar**Therefore at that time
> when all the people heard the sound of the cornet, flute,
> harp, sackbut, psaltery, and all kinds of musick, all the
> people, the nations, and the languages, fell down and
> worshipped the golden image that Nebuchadnezzar the
> king had set up.

The proclamation told them to fall down and worship. The
completed action is indicated in the past tense of the verb—
they *fell down.*

This whole chapter is excellent for reading practice.

When reading selections from the Bible in which God is
quoted, visualize the qualities God represents to you and your
tone will follow your thought. A long pause before starting such
direct discourse helps to give value to what is said. Watch that
you stay behind his words as you read. Do not use circumflex

or decided change of pitch. The more simply a passage is read the more profound it will be to the listener.

In a book called *A Day in Athens* it is related that a young orator came to Socrates and wanted the great teacher to criticize his oration. When the young man had finished speaking, the philosopher said, "Young man, break open your words and get inside of them." Most of us need that advice in reading. We are outside of our words instead of fully identifying ourselves with them. We are too tame, too lukewarm. We should give ourselves completely to the words, or rather, to the ideas for which they stand. We need to be possessed with them. Try reading these verses and wholly entering into the words as you read:

> Behold, what manner of love the Father hath bestowed upon us, that we should be called the sons of God: therefore the world knoweth us not, because it knew him not. Beloved, now are we the sons of God, and it doth not yet appear what we shall be: but we know that, when he shall appear, we shall be like him; for we shall see him as he is. And every man that hath this hope in him purifieth himself, even as he is pure.—I JOHN 3:1-3

The first word, *behold,* occurs about 1,300 times in the Bible and is like a sore thumb to many readers. This is because it is only a word and not a thought to them. Its meaning varies. The original Greek from which this word was translated also means *consider, be aware of, understand.* Think of a word in modern language which could be substituted for *behold,* and use the same tone to say *behold* as you might use in saying the modern word. The meaning of this verse seems to give this pattern:

> Behold . . , what manner (of) love the Father hath bestowed upon us . . , (that) we (should be) called the sons (of) God . . . : **ch** therefore [for this reason] the world knoweth (us not), because (it knew) him (not) . . . . . **ch**

⌊Beloved, now (are we the sons of God) . . . ,ꟻ (and it doth
not yet) appear (what we shall be): but we know that,
when) he (shall appear), (we shall be) like him . . ; (for we
shall) see him as he is . . . . And every (man) that hath this
hope (in him) purifieth himself, even (as) he [God] (is
pure).

In the expression *every man,* if *man* were emphasized, it
might exclude the women and children. It should be said as you
say *everyone,* the emphasis on *every.*

Do not let the parentheses such as "now (are we the sons of
God)," cause you to break the phrases.

Did you think of the ideas back of the words as you read
these verses? If not, try reading them again and go through
each important word for the fullest meaning you know. *You
must not allow this study to turn you to the letter and cause you
to lose the spirit of what you read.*

A man who had used this book to help him with public reading, had not studied it thoroughly enough, so he vehemently
hit every word that was underlined in the transcriptions. Of
course this overemphasis led to distorted reading. Again let
me urge you to visualize the underlined words, see their relation
to what has already been read, but do not give them artificial
emphasis. Work until the words disappear and only ideas exist
as you read. You will not accomplish this through thoughtless
rereading. Always be listening through the words as you practice. The moment you catch yourself reading words without
thinking, stop.

You have been advised to read a word at a time, not to look
ahead and scatter your thought. But you have also been told
that in reading a series which builds up to a climax, any repetition is slighted until you reach the last member of the group,
the climax. Here all parts are again valued and often given

with a slower tempo. You will naturally think, "How can I know which is the last of a series if I do not look ahead?" When you find yourself in a series, look ahead, but not *as* you are reading. It is at the pause between ideas that you glance on to see how far the series runs. You do not try to determine the meaning of the words, only the length of the series. This quick look is comparable to the way one places the lines of a tennis court before making a shot, but keeps his eye on the ball at the instant he strokes it.

Experiment in determining the length of a series in this verse from I Chronicles 29:11:

> Thine, O Lord, is the greatness, and the power, and the glory, and the victory, and the majesty: for all that is in the heaven and in the earth is thine; thine is the kingdom, O Lord, and thou art exalted as head above all.

When you get to *power* and see another *and,* you know that you are in a series. You take time enough at the pause to glance ahead and see how long the series runs. *And the* is thrown away before *glory,* and even more rapidly before *victory,* but it is re-valued before *majesty,* this phrase being the climax. It will read like this:

> Thine, ⌊O Lord, (is the) greatness, and (the) power, (and the) glory, ᴴ(and the) ⌊victory, and the majesty; for all (that is) in the heaven (and in the) earth (is thine); (thine is the) kingdom, ⌊(O Lord) , and thou are exalted as head above all.

Ah and *O* are human sounds; they give an insincere effect if they are said as words. In nondramatic reading they may be given time but not emphasis. "O Lord, how great are thy works!" Notice the effect that is produced if *O* is emphasized.

But if it is given time and said thoughtfully without emphasis, it adds depth of feeling.

It has been urged that you let the inspiration of the idea back of the words take care of the color and quality of the voice. This can come with the first reading as well as after many repetitions. However, if you think you are only able to grasp the meaning after several rereadings, you will have to use this method for you must get to the underlying thought.

It is sometimes difficult to read selections where personal pronouns are used to refer to two different characters. When the pronoun does not refer to the person in thought it must be emphasized, for it introduces a different character. An example of this is in Genesis 32:24-30:

And Jacob was left alone . . . . ; and there wrestled (a man with him) (until the) breaking (of the) day. (And when he) saw that he prevailed not against him, he touched the hollow (of his) thigh;   (and the hollow of Jacob's thigh was) out of joint (as he wrestled with him). L(And he said) . . . . , Let me go, (for the) day breaketh. And he (said) . . . , I will not (let thee go), (except thou) bless me . . . . (And he said unto him) . . . , What is thy name . . ?

And he said . . . , Jacob . . (And he) said . . . . , Thy name shall be called no more Jacob, but Israel: for as a prince (hast thou) power with God (and with) men, (and hast) prevailed . . . . And Jacob asked him, and said . . . . , Tell me,   (I pray thee), thy name . . . (And he said) . . . , Wherefore is it (that thou dost) ask (after my) name . . . . ? (And he) blessed him there . . . . And Jacob called the name of

the place Peniel . . . . . : (for I have) seen God face to
face. . . . . , ⌊ (and my) life (is) preserved.

Although a personal pronoun is rarely emphasized, at times
an idea is made specific by emphasis, as *ye* in the following
verse. II Corinthians 6:16:

And what agreement (hath the) temple (of) God (with)
idols . . ? for ye (are the temple of the living God); ⏋ (As
God hath) said . . . , I will dwell (in them), (and) walk (in
them); (and I will be) their God, and they (shall be) my
people.

They is emphasized because it is a contrast to *I*.
Another example is in Matthew 7:7-11.

com Ask . . , (and it shall be) given you . . ; seek . . , (and
ye shall) find . . ; knock, (and it shall be) opened (unto
you) . . . : [The truth is now generalized with:] For every
(one that asketh) receiveth; and he that seeketh findeth;
and to him that knocketh (it shall be) opened. [Now it is
made specific and for this reason the personal pronoun is
stressed.]   (Or what man is there of) you, whom (if his) son
ask bread, (will he give him a) stone? (Or if he ask a) fish,
⏋ (will he give him a) serpent? If ye then, being evil, know
how to give good gifts unto your children . . . , ⑀ how much
more shall your Father (which is in) heaven (give good
things to them that ask) him?

Here is a selection which is frequently read emphasizing *is*.
It is transcribed to show the greater dignity and depth of
meaning when this emphasis is not made. Isaiah 45:5-6.

Correct: I am (the) Lord [Supreme Ruler] . . , (and there is)

none else., (there is) no God <u>beside</u> (me) ....: [tenderly]

(I) girded thee, though thou (hast) not known (me): (that)

they may know (from the) rising (of the) sun, and from

(the) <u>west,</u> (that there is none beside me) .... (I am the)

<u>Lord</u>, (and there is) none else.

The last two phrases are repeated with no new idea. This is done for emphasis, of course, so there is even more value given to the illustrative words *Lord* and *none else* than when they are first introduced. They are often misread in this way:

Incorrect: (I) <u>am</u> the Lord, and there <u>is</u> none else, there is no God beside <u>me</u>.

An example of lost continuity is often heard in the reading of the first two verses of Romans 8:1-2. You hear this emphasis:

Incorrect: There <u>is</u> therefore now no condemnation to them which are in Christ Jesus, who walk not after the flesh, but <u>after</u> the ⌊ Spirit. For the law/of the Spirit-of-life in <u>Christ</u> Jesus hath made me free/from the law of sin/and death.⟍

Law is the new idea in the second sentence. Because this sentence has been so frequently read with the wrong phrasing, "the-Spirit-of-life," see that *law* goes with *Spirit* and that the words *life in Christ Jesus* go together.

Correct: There is <u>therefore</u> now no condemnation to them which are in Christ Jesus, who <u>walk</u> not after the flesh, (but after the) <u>Spirit</u> .... (For the) <u>law</u> (of the spirit) of life (in Christ Jesus) hath made (me) <u>free</u> (from the law of) sin and death.

In the second sentence, the word *spirit* would not be incorrectly emphasized if it had been visualized properly in the first sentence.

Although simple negatives are not ordinarily emphasized, here is an example where *neither, nor,* and *no* are valued because they are the new idea words:

> And as <u>Jesus</u> passed by, he saw a man (which was) blind (from his) <u>birth</u> . . . (And his) <u>disciples</u> asked him, saying . . . , Master, who did sin, this man, (or his) <u>parents</u>, (that he was) <u>born</u> blind . . . ? Jesus answered . . . , Neither (hath this man sinned), <u>nor</u> (his parents): (but that the) works of <u>God</u> (should be) made manifest in him. I must <u>work</u> (the works of) him that sent me, (while it is) day: the <u>night</u> cometh, when <u>no</u> (man can work.)—JOHN 9:1-4

An example of a negative which is emphasized for contrast is:

Correct: <u>Beware</u> lest any man spoil (you) through philosophy (and) vain <u>deceit</u>, after (the) <u>tradition</u> (of) <u>men</u>, (after the) rudiment (of the) <u>world</u>, and <u>not</u> (after) <u>Christ</u>.

> —COLOSSIANS 2:8

An example of the added strength which comes into reading as it is kept conversational shows in Isaiah 54:17. It is often read this way:

Incorrect: No weapon that is formed against <u>thee</u> shall ∟<u>prosper</u>; and <u>every</u> ∟tongue that shall rise against <u>thee</u> is ∟judgment <u>thou</u> shalt ∟condemn. This is the heritage of the servants of the ∟Lord, and their righteousness (is of) <u>me</u>, <u>saith</u> the ∟Lord.

The conversational pattern is like this:

Correct: No <u>weapon</u> (that is) formed against thee (sh'll) <u>prosper</u>; (and) every <u>tongue</u> (that shall) rise (against thee) in judgment thou (shalt) <u>condemn</u> . . . . (This is the) <u>heritage</u> (of

the) servants (of the) Lord . . , (and their) righteousness (is)
of me, saith the Lord.

In bringing continuity into the reading through slighting
repetitions, it is not necessarily the same word which is slighted
but it may be one of its synonyms, as in Psalms 33:6-9:

> By the word (of the) Lord (were the) heavens made; and
> all (the) host (of them) (by the breath of his mouth). He
> gathereth (the) waters (of the) sea together (as an) heap:
> (he) layeth up (the depth) in storehouses. Let all the earth
> fear (the Lord): (let all the) inhabitants (of the) world
> (stand in awe of him). (For he) spake, (and it was) done;
> (he) commanded, (and it) stood fast.

By the breath of his mouth gives the same idea as by the word
of the Lord, so it is thrown away when it is read; also the depth
because it carries the same meaning as the waters of the sea.

An interesting example of the rhythm which comes into reading through good visualizing is found in Matthew 7:17-20:

> Even so every good tree bringeth forth good fruit; but a
> corrupt tree bringeth forth evil fruit. A good tree cannot
> bring forth evil fruit, neither can a corrupt tree bring forth
> good fruit. Every tree that bringeth not forth good fruit is
> hewn down, and cast into the fire. Wherefore by their fruits
> ye shall know them.

See if your reading sounded like this pattern:

> Every good tree bringeth forth (good) fruit; (but a) corrupt
> (tree) (bringeth forth) evil (fruit). (A good tree) cannot
> (bring forth) evil fruit, (neither can a) corrupt (tree) bring
> forth good fruit . . . . Wherefore (by their) fruits (ye shall)
> know (them).

The real meaning is hidden in the following passage when it is read in a mournful way. Value the action verbs in it. This makes it happen as you read instead of sounding like a mere rehearsal of events of another time.

Correct: For this corruptible must put on incorruption, and this mortal (must put on) immortality . . . . So when (this corruptible shall have put on incorruption), (and this mortal shall have put on immortality) . , then (shall be) brought to pass the saying (that is) written . . . . , Death is swallowed up (in) victory.—I CORINTHIANS 15:53, 54

The last word, *victory,* needs to be lifted almost bodily to avoid the old resigned mood in which it is usually read:

Incorrect: Death is swallowed up in ∟victory.

By throwing away the repetition and valuing only the new thoughts, you show the continuity in these verses:

For ye see your calling, ∟(brethren), how that not many wise men after the flesh . . , (not many) mighty, not many noble, (are) called . . . . : (But) God hath chosen the foolish things (of the world) to confound (the wise) . . ; ∟(and God hath chosen the) weak (things of the world to confound the things which are) mighty; and base (things of the world), (and things which are) despised, (hath God chosen), yea, (and things which) are not, to bring to nought (things that) are . . : that no flesh should glory (in) his presence.

—I CORINTHIANS 1:26-29

One who does not understand this law of continuity and yet is a good reader is like the person who plays the piano by ear but has no understanding of harmony. Many times he makes very pleasing music, but there are occasions when the harmony eludes him and he has nothing to fall back on; he does not know the science as well as the art of his music. However, the music of the person who plays by ear alone is usually more acceptable than mechanically perfect playing void of inspiration. The one who understands the science, i.e., the principles and rules underlying what he does, and still has not lost his spontaneity and satisfaction in playing, or reading, is the true artist.

Tempo is indicated, as usual, in this citation by S for slower and F for faster.

> Woe unto him that striveth (with his) Maker . . . ! **F** Let the potsherd (strive with the potsherds of the) earth. (Shall the) clay say (to him that) fashioneth it . . . , **S** What makest thou . ? **F** For thy work . . , **S** He hath no hands . ? (Woe unto him that saith unto his) father . . , **S** What begettest thou . . ? **F** (or to the) woman . . , **S** (What hast) thou (brought forth) . . . . ? **S** Thus saith the Lord, the Holy One of Israel, (and his) Maker . . , Ask me of things to come concerning my sons, and (concerning the work of my hands) command ye me. I have made the earth, and created man upon it: **L** I, even my hands, have stretched out the heavens, and all their host (have I commanded) . . . . I have raised him up in righteousness . . , (and I will) direct all his ways.—ISAIAH 45:9-13

A good example of building up to a climax is found in Genesis 3:6. The numbers placed before the phrases are used to indicate the different levels, so that you will not start with so much intensity that you cannot make a climax of the last. Do not read the numbers.

The serpent is tempting Eve to eat of the apple that was in the midst of the garden.

And when the woman saw [1] (that the) tree was good for food, [2] **F**(and that it was) pleasant (to the) eyes, [3] (and a tree to be) desired to make one wise, (she) took (of the fruit thereof), and did eat, and gave also (unto her) husband with her; and he (did eat).

Other such examples:

And thou shalt love the Lord thy God [1] with all thy heart, [2] and (with all thy) soul, [3] **F**(and with all thy) mind, [4] and with all thy strength: (this is the) first commandment.—MARK 12:30

[1] Now will I rise.., saith the Lord..; [2] (now will I be) exalted; [3] now will I lift up myself.—ISAIAH 33:10

[1] For the Lord (is) our judge, [2] (the Lord is our) lawgiver, [3] the Lord is (our) king; he will save us.

—ISAIAH 33:22

Be sure to visualize *king*. The thought of this word is usually lost in reading this verse because of the tendency to let go of last words mentally. *Our* is often given more emphasis than *king*.

A beautiful example of contrast is found in Matthew 7:24-27.

Therefore whosoever heareth these sayings of mine, (and) doeth (them), (I will) liken him (unto a) wise man, which built (his) house (upon a) rock: [See the next happen, as you say it.] And the rain descended, (and the) floods came, **L**(and the) winds blew, (and) beat (upon that house); (and it) fell not: (for it was) founded (upon a) rock.

(And every one that heareth these sayings of mine, and doeth them) not, (shall be likened unto a) foolish (man),

(which built) <u>his</u> (house upon the) <u>sand</u>: [Your tone in the
next phrase should imply, "As I said before—"] (And the
rain descended), (and the floods came), (and the winds
blew), (and beat upon) <u>that</u> (house); (and) <u>it</u> f<u>e</u>ll . . . . . :
Sand gre<u>a</u>t (was the) fa<u>l</u>l (of it).

The careless reader falls into certain set patterns in his reading. He almost invariably raises his voice at commas, and drops
it with the last word, regardless of the sense. With two words
in the same construction, he raises his tone on the first and
drops it on the second, even though a well-written selection will
usually have the more important word last. These mistakes are
conspicuous in the reading of the last verses of Jude. Be careful to think only of the meaning of the word you are saying.

Now unto him that is able to keep you from fa<u>l</u>ling, and to

present you <u>faultless</u> before the pre<u>s</u>ence of his glo<u>r</u>y with

exceeding <u>joy</u>, to the only wise G<u>o</u>d our Sav<u>i</u>our, be glory

(and) m<u>a</u>jesty, dom<u>i</u>nion (and) po<u>w</u>er, both n<u>o</u>w (and) <u>e</u>ver.

The pairs of words are incorrectly read, *glory and majesty,*
dominion and power; the important last words, *falling, joy,*
ever, are not thought through, so the tone is dropped as they
are said.

There is a tendency to stress or sing modifying words, especially vivid ones, at the expense of the nouns or verbs they
modify. We hear:

Incorrect: . . . shall ge<u>n</u>tly lead those that are with young.

—ISAIAH 40:11

Correct: . . . shall gently le<u>a</u>d th<u>o</u>se (that are with) yo<u>u</u>ng.

The fact that the word *gently* could be omitted and the sentence
still give the meaning, should show you that this word is less
important than *lead.*

The word *all* is one which is sung by a large majority every time it is read.

Incorrect: Count it a-a-l-l/joy when ye fall into divers temptations; knowing/(this), that the trying/of your faith ⌊worketh ⌊patience.—JAMES 1:2, 3

Correct: Count it all joy when ye fall into divers temptations; knowing this, that the trying (of your) faith worketh patience.

Because the listener does not know what *all* modifies when it is first read, it means nothing to him until he hears the word *joy.*

When *all* is used as a summing up, it should be given a positive stress, but not a singing inflection. An example of this is:

Vanity of vanities, saith the Preacher, vanity of vanities; all (is vanity).—ECCLESIASTES 1:2

In Psalms 34:17 and 19, *all* is used in both the stressed and unstressed forms:

The righteous cry, and the Lord heareth, and delivereth them out of all their troubles . . [Do not stress all here.] Many are the afflictions (of the righteous): but the Lord (delivereth him out of them) all.

With generalities, the qualifying adjective is often stressed, as *everybody, everyone, every man, every place, everything, all men, all things, anyone, any man, any place.*

Correct: See that none render evil for evil unto any (man); but ever follow that which is good, both among yourselves, and to all (men).—I THESSALONIANS 5:15

For all (things) are for your sakes, that the abundant grace might through the thanksgiving of many redound to the glory of God.—II CORINTHIANS 4:15

> And <u>every</u> man that hath this hope in him purifieth him-
> self . . . . —I JOHN 3:3

To read two related comparisons, read the first as if it stood alone. In the second throw away the comparison which has been established in thought, and bring out the new idea in both members of the second comparison. Thus: <u>My</u> <u>car</u> is <u>larger</u> than <u>your</u> (car) because (my) <u>family</u> (is larger than) your <u>family</u>. Another example is Isaiah 55:8,9.

> For <u>my</u> thoughts are not <u>your</u> (thoughts), neither (are your)
> <u>ways</u> (my) ways, saith the Lord. For as the heavens are
> <u>higher</u> than the <u>earth</u>, so are my ways (higher than) <u>your</u>
> ways, (and my) <u>thoughts</u> (than) your <u>thoughts</u>.

One of the most difficult problems in Bible reading lies in the many repetitions. Understanding the science and art of conversational reading helps you to read them with sincerity and still avoid monotony. It has been stated that we never alter tone for the sake of variation, but that the tone changes as a result of the thinking. In writing there is a rather general rule used for a series, called the 2, 3, 1 rule. The second in importance is placed first, the less important items next, and the most momentous last. Ordinarily a certain amount of building up occurs in any series. In reading this build-up is not necessarily accomplished by a continuous raising of the pitch. Often the second phrase comes in at a lower level than the first. Then the third will come in from a higher level, as if one said, "Not only that, but *this*." Let us consider that bane of many Bible readers, Philippians 4:8:

> Finally, brethren, whatsoever things are true, whatsoever
> things are honest, whatsoever things are just, whatsoever
> things are pure, whatsoever things are lovely, whatsoever
> things are of good report; if there be any virtue, and if
> there be any praise, think on these things.

Finally is positive. In the first phrase of the series each important word is established. The next phrase starts at a lower level and slights the repetition, *honest* being the only new thought in this. The next throws away the repetition even more rapidly, and visualizes *just* with a low, strong tone quality. In such a long repetition, you will feel the need of re-establishing the word *things* by giving it a little time in the phrase, *whatsoever things are pure.* The quickest tempo in the verse comes in the next phrase, *whatsoever things are lovely.* Also the accumulative sense brings it to the highest pitch. The last and most important comes in slowly and impressively, as if it were played with a full organ. The word *whatsoever* is almost syllabled as it is said. *Virtue* is the next word of importance. *Virtue* is translated from a Greek word meaning *manliness, excellence, stronger for lifting. Praise* is the next new-idea word. Then comes the most important word of the passage, *think.* The rest is already in the picture and does not need valuing. Many want to value *these.* When asked why, they will say, "We should think on *these* things instead of things which are untrue, dishonest, etc." But there is no such contrast in this verse. It pictures only the things that are true, honest, just, pure, lovely, of good report. Then comes the big point, *"think* on these things."

> Finally, (brethren), whatsoever things (are) true, L(whatsoever things are) honest, H (whatsoever things are) L just, (whatsoever things are) pure, F (whatsoever things are) lovely, S what-so-ever things (are of) good report, (if there be any) virtue, (and if there be any) praise, think (on these things).

Make no break between *think* and the following phrase.

Another difficult repetition is I Kings 3:11. Solomon had asked that God give him an understanding heart to judge His people.

And God said unto him . . . . . , Because thou (hast) asked
(this thing), (and hast) _not_ (asked for) thyself long life;
neither (hast asked) _riches_ (for thyself), nor (hast asked the)
life (of) thine _enemies;_ S but _hast_ _asked_ for thyself _under-_
standing (to) _discern_ _judgment;_ Behold, (I have) _done_
(according to thy words): lo, (I have) _given_ (thee a wise
and an understanding heart); (so that there was) none like
thee _before_ (thee), neither _after_ (thee shall any arise) like
unto thee. (And I have) _also_ (given thee that which thou
hast) _not_ (asked), both riches, (and) honour: F (so that
there shall not be) any among the _kings_ like unto thee all
thy days.

PART III

POISE
ITS RELATION TO POSTURE AND PLATFORM WORK

Chapter 15

POISE

The calmness and assurance which the world calls *poise* arises from a mental balance and cannot be put on like a robe. A divine quality, this balance—not too much and not too little.

Dorothy Maynor, noted soprano, gave a striking example of the power of poise at one of her appearances in the Hollywood Bowl. The symphony accompanied her first selections, next she was accompanied by the piano; lastly she came out onto the stage alone and took her place by the curve of the piano. For an interminable time she quietly stood there. The people were restive, unused to the enforced pause, uncertain what was expected of them. There was desultory applause. Still she waited until there was a breathless silence. Then she sang, unaccompanied, "Were You There When They Crucified My Lord?" The words hung in the stillness of the night air, disembodied, with a purity which brought unchecked tears. At the end of the song she again stood for, I would say, two minutes—an eternity to keep twenty thousand people quiet. This time there was no applause. When she left the stage the people walked out, chastened and subdued. Somehow she had forced us to come face to face with ourselves—a soul-searching experience.

My explanation of this phenomenon would be: First, she was technically prepared. She knew the song perfectly. She knew that she could sing and sing well—she had a right valuation of her ability. But she also knew how to listen. She listened, both to quiet self-consciousness and to reach the essence of the song right at that moment. She listened until she was filled with its inspiration, until nothing existed to her but the song. She valued it so highly that she would not let a sound, a rustle, interfere with its expression. It became an active force and everyone there, including herself, was on tiptoe of expectation. Then the song emerged with its own motor power, impersonal, magnificent.

The skeptical may say, "How do you know that wasn't a carefully studied technique and not sincere listening at all?" My answer is that there are certain truths which you know intuitively. While the need of a pause before starting such a sensitive song could have been decided beforetime, it was her poise at the time of the performance which enabled her to pause in that selfless way. She could not have lifted the audience to such heights by means of a technical trick alone.

Poise comes to you *when you turn away from the thought of persons, including yourself, and become interested in ideas.*

When ideas fill your thought you grow eloquent in expression, keen in business, inspired in the arts. What you do contains the aura of the idea and is free from the petty and personal.

When you let your thought become divided, thinking partly about the effect you are making, or of your inability or ability, you are likely to become tense and unnatural. You may find yourself giving that "hope-you-approve-of-me" smile, or casting furtive glances to see what impression you are making. You must have integrity to retain poise, a positive position which is not concerned with what others think about you but is wholly at the service of the idea you are expressing.

The synonyms for poise, given by students from time to time, will help you to understand it, while its antonyms show you the traits which indicate a lack of poise.

POISE

equality	inequality
brother	inferiority, superiority

ease	labored
rhythm	ponderous
decision	unable to say "no"
firmness	easy going
mastery over self	drifting
moral courage	timidity
build one's house on a rock	wheel of fortune
having all one's wits about one	infatuation
unprejudiced	biased
serenity	stirred up
	impetuosity
well-balanced	go off on a tangent
unoffended	irritable

With poise you retain your power of decision, you can say "no" firmly and without apology or explanation, and yet be courteous. You cannot do this if you feel resentful or apologetic, but it is easy if you keep your thought on the reason for your decision. However, this does not mean that an arbitrary stand is desirable. I have noticed that the truly great do not strain to be consistent in a stubborn or self-righteous way. They are far more concerned in reaching truth than in proving themselves to be correct.

An apt example of poise is that of a skilled high diver just before he goes into action. He is perfectly quiet, but not static. Everything about him looks alert and controlled. He is listening for and valuing the dive he is about to make—in other words, selecting and visualizing it, whether it be a swan dive, a jackknife, or a double somersault—and if he has retained his poise he springs into its execution with precision.

The same method will work for you. Listen for the idea you are about to express, see it as clearly as the high diver sees his prospective dive. Then you will move into its expression with the nicety which idea-direction gives.

There is an exact balance in poise, just as there is in listening—a firmness which is not swayed by passing notions, by dispositional tendencies, by fear of what someone thinks; a firmness balanced with a yielding to the idea, a flexibility of thought and body, a freedom from unnecessary restraint. Someone described a poised person as being like a weighted doll, the kind that springs back when you knock it over, nonresistant because he knows that he can immediately resume an upright position if he should be pushed over.

Unoffended gives a quality of poise—one which the oversensitive person needs to recognize. The Chinese say, "He who forgets a blow suffers nothing; he who remembers it, strikes himself many times."

Will Rogers was at ease with anyone from a bootblack to the President of the United States. His outlook of equality, as well as his kindliness and appreciation for others, gave him real poise. It helped me to understand his attitude when I found that the word *brother* is a synonym of *poise,* while *inferiority* and *superiority* are its antonyms. Many times when I have felt uncomfortable among certain people, thinking of this word *brother* has made me feel that I could meet them on the same level and speak to them man to man.

Inferiority has been generally accepted as a lack of poise, but few have realized that *superiority* is in the same group of antonyms. Often the condescending businessman, the supercilious salesperson, the sophisticated socialite, are regarded as examples of poise. In fact, some books and courses of study recommend this lofty attitude as effective for executives because it puts others on the defensive. But should a manner which takes away the dignity and power of decision from another be a worthy aim? A sense of superiority builds a barrier between you and the ones with whom you deal. You lose the easy feeling which you have with your own, and as a result those around you become constrained and do not express themselves freely.

The person with real poise is gracious toward everyone he

meets. A teacher of etiquette once said, "A lady handles every-thing as if it were the only one of its kind in existence." I would like to extend this attitude and say, "A gentleman, as well as a lady, treats every person he meets as if he were the only one of his kind in existence." In fact he is. Many times I have been greatly enriched by someone whose personality was at first unattractive to me, when I was able to maintain my poise, my "brother" attitude toward him.

Does this chapter help you to figure out why you have felt ill at ease in certain situations?

Were you fully focused upon what you were doing or were you halfhearted because your thought was scattered? Half-heartedness makes you vague, hesitant, or superficial. "Eye on the ball," not dreamy absentness, is necessary for poise. Did you have a feeling of *brother* toward those about you, or one of inferiority? When you feel at a disadvantage, you may catch yourself trying to "make an impression." This is futile for it is *what you think of yourself,* not what others think of you, which makes you feel inferior. Or did you feel superior, and let this dampen your spontaneity by a condescending attitude? "Be yourself."

Were you afraid that someone was criticizing you or were you so interested in ideas that you forgot about persons? Your concern should not be about what others are thinking, but about what you yourself are thinking.

Was there rhythm, naturalness, and beauty in what you did, or was your action marred, either because you hurried and jumped into things impetuously, or because you were burdened with responsibility and became halting or pedantic.

Every genius has poise at the time of his performance. Whether he be a speaker, a prizefighter, an actor, or a reader, he is vitally aware of the idea back of his activity. This awareness takes care of the situation. Self is forgotten and the idea holds everything about him in conscious control and makes him move in a smooth, directed way.

Try this attitude yourself in the minor happenings of the day, until the ease of action which accompanies true poise becomes natural to you on all occasions.

Chapter *16*

POSTURE

The world may say that passing years cause stooped shoulders, crooked backs, hanging heads and stiff joints. Don't believe it! Bad posture and awkward movements are much more likely to come from rushing, or from laziness, discouragement, a burdened feeling, really from temperamental tendencies. The continual strain of hurrying causes you to grow tense and tight in different parts of the body, especially through the shoulders and back of the neck; or an easygoing disposition tempts you to sprawl in your chair self-indulgently instead of controlling your posture; or you may become stooped from carrying mental loads.

The first corrective is suggested in the preceding chapter—a right sense of poise, a mental balance. Then if you learn the natural position of your bony structure you can go about correcting some of the bad posture habits which may have crept up on you.

Your first aim is a straight back. Point the sitting bones toward the ground, the upper end of the spine to the sky. This adjustment straightens the back, keeps the buttocks in, brings the abdomen up and back and the legs together and a little forward. Let the legs remain that way. This is their natural position. To force them to be directly under you makes the knees stiff, throws the whole body out of line, and leads to what is known as a sway-back. Try to stand with the legs directly under the body, then put one hand on the abdomen and one on the back, well below the waist, bend the knees slightly, and you will feel the back straighten and the body adjust itself.

Another helpful way of bringing the body into correct position is to lift the chest and feel that the rest of the body hangs easily from it. Watch that the shoulders are down and the knees easy.

To correct round shoulders and a heavy neck, push the top of your head against an imaginary ceiling a couple of inches above your ordinary height. Take all the slack out of your posture. Lift the head up—push against that ceiling. Don't let it settle down between the shoulders. Now push down with your shoulders, as if you were carrying a heavy suitcase in each hand. Feel the head up, the shoulders down—not back but straight down. Your coat may not fit you now but hold the posture because it is natural and right, and have your coat altered. Your dresses may be two or three inches too long in back with this better posture. Also your waist is sure to be smaller. Men often have to tighten their belt when they correct their standing and walking position in this way.

Once you establish right posture any activity can become a good slimming exercise.

Walking is an idea. Anything which helps you to see the idea will improve your technique. Imagine walking downhill beside a rapidly flowing stream. Think of the qualities of the moving water and bring these into your walk. There is a swift smoothness, strength, rhythm, lilt. It is a pleasure to feel as if you are swinging along abreast of the stream keeping in step with its free, natural motion and unbroken continuity. Perfect co-ordination can come involuntarily as you move with an idea.

An actor who has for many years played distinguished roles in motion pictures was seen standing in a local village bank, mopping his face with his handkerchief as though hot and weary; but when he walked out there was no slump or heaviness in his movements. His true poise and fine posture were not upset by little irritations. His walk was not histrionic. It merely had the beauty of a thing simply done—an inevitable rightness.

The natives in the South Seas walk like kings and queens, smoothly and rhythmically. It is said that carrying burdens on their heads helps to give this steadiness. Try to get the feel of pushing up against a loaded basket by placing your hand on your head as you walk. Take hold of the ground with your feet and stretch the body up against an imaginary load. With good visualization you can almost achieve the actual experience.

To walk with music, either imagined or really heard, brings buoyancy into the step and does away with labored or heavy trudging. Have you ever been weary and then heard beautiful or stirring music and felt as if it picked you up and moved you along in its rhythm? You cease to realize that you are carrying your own weight. Fatigue disappears as thought becomes filled with the music.

One effective method of learning to walk freely is to have someone take hold of your clothing a little above the front of the waist, at your solar plexus, and pull you forward, walking beside you. You can even take hold of your own clothing and have the feel that all parts of your body—legs, arms, and head —move from the one point. Resist the pull slightly at the waist so that you feel yourself being drawn forward from the center. Then walk to the rhythm of saying, "Two long legs—, two long legs—," taking a step with each word and at the pause between the phrases. Imagine that your legs go clear to this central point. If you are doing it correctly, labor disappears from your walk and you move with an idea, not with feet and many parts. Should you have the habit of letting the head hang forward, the chin floating, the shoulders drooping, you will find that resisting this pull from the center brings the head up, the chin in, straightens the back, and brings balance and unity throughout the body. Do not let this method cause you to lean backwards. The three main parts of the body, the head, chest, and hip girdle, should line up vertically.

Many salesmen, in their effort to "get their man," hurry,

leading with the head. It is difficult for them to slow up enough
to get the feel of effortless action which this way of walking
brings. In classes they are usually two jumps ahead of the one
trying to lead them. One man tried for several minutes to get
this rhythm. He was walked back and forth in the classroom to
"Two long legs—" but still he could not slow up enough to
let himself be drawn. Finally he grasped the idea, and the whole
class exclaimed at the change which came over him. He took on
a look of dignity, the look of a man who would be sought, not
one who would be running after his client. Everything about
him expressed importance. This walk was not put on from the
outside. The self-disciplining which he had to do before he
could walk correctly actually produced a mental poise which
expressed itself in a fine bearing.

Notice that "Two long legs—" is not "Two long *steps*." The
length of step is determined by the height of the individual
and the rate of speed at which he is walking. Rhythm is broken
if either too long or too short steps are taken. Short men often
take long steps, seeming to feel this will make them look taller.
The opposite is the case, for as they stretch out horizontally
with their long strides they appear shorter. A quick nervous
person finds it difficult to slow down to his correct rhythm and
often takes short quick steps. Listen inwardly, and the right
length of step will come to you, whether you are entering a
platform where you need to be unhurried and dignified, or
walking briskly in the mountains.

If you are short, you look noticeably taller as you walk in
this way. Still, the height of the tall person is not exaggerated
by it. Instead, he looks well-balanced. If you are tall, do not
stand and walk bent over or crouched down in the effort to look
shorter. Stand tall, enjoy your height. If you keep a right sense
of value of yourself, your stature will look just right for you
and will command respect. If you are sensitive about your
stature, you will appear awkward.

The shoulders need to be broadened and to swing easily, not to be forced back in a strained position, or drooped forward in a dejected, helpless way. The arms should not swing in a military fashion. Neither should they flop around in abandonment. Let them move in obedience to the natural swing of the body. Notice the slight amount of movement which a child makes with his arms when walking. In hiking and climbing, one man found that when he did not swing his arms excessively, he moved with more precision, not overjumping his mark when going over rocks.

Do not turn the toes out. The Indian method of walking with the feet straight is most efficient. If you could see slow-motion pictures of someone walking with the toes turned out, you would notice that he swings first to one side, then to the other, following the line of the feet. This walk is not far removed from a waddle.

Another bad habit is that of walking with the feet apart. To correct this, think of moving in one straight line, not two.

The head should be held straight. To hold it on one side gives a weak, effeminate look. This is often done unconsciously. It is a mannerism and detracts from your appearance.

The chin pushed out and up like Mussolini's, gives an effect of pride; the chin held in, a look of suspicious caution, characteristic of lawyers, always wary lest they say anything incriminating. On the other hand, just as leading with the chin is a dangerous habit in prizefighting, so in everyday life people who are dreamers, impractical or negative, tend to have a posture of weakly floating chin and drooping shoulders. This quality of thought is likely to get it "on the chin."

Think of the finest things you know about yourself. Then appreciate those who are around you, and your head and chin should be in a good position. If you think of how right you are and how mistaken others are, then the chin gets too high. If you dwell on your inferiority or on how misunderstood you are, the shoulders are likely to droop. But a right valuation of yourself and of others is an immediate aid to good posture.

Sit high. Try to make the whole backbone touch the back of the chair. This helps to keep the abdomen up and the back straight. To push down with the elbows straightens the shoulders and raises the chest.

In rising, feel that you are drawn up by a wire attached to your chest. This eliminates effort. In an auditorium, don't pull yourself up by the seat in front of you or push yourself up by the arms of a chair. Both of these actions give a look of age and heaviness. Move with thought, not brawn. To rise from a low, soft chair, slide forward and sit at an angle to the edge. Then you can get up easily. In any group in which it is necessary to rise frequently, if you have a low seat stay in this forward position; do not settle back and have to shove yourself forward each time you rise.

Keep the torso easily erect both in rising and sitting down. In sitting down do not lean over so that the head is much farther forward than the feet. Men often do this because they are pulling up the knees of their trousers. If you are on a platform make this adjustment after being seated.

Let go with your hands. Let them be quiet. Hands give you away. Restless fingers are often the one detracting feature on a person who otherwise appears perfectly poised. Avoid toying with anything or clutching the wrist of one hand with the other. Refuse to feel that you must be grasping something. When sitting, if I feel self-conscious about my hands I find it helpful to let them lie in my lap, fingers up, one hand resting in the other, or the upper hand palm down with the fingers stretched out in the palm of the other hand. A man may be more comfortable with one hand resting easily on each leg, palms down, or with one of them resting on the arm of his chair. Let them be still until there is a call for action on their part. Then they will move in response to your thought.

Women should watch to keep their knees together when seated. The knees may be crossed on occasion, the platform excepted. Turn sideways when you do this, however, so that the swinging foot is not toward the center of the room. If you should be too fleshy to keep the knees together or to cross them, turn slightly in your chair and keep the forward leg straight from the knee down, the foot flat on the floor. Let the other knee separate as much as is necessary, but keep the feet together.

In entering a room filled with people, pause a moment in the doorway and listen. Do not go into the room and then falter self-consciously because you are not certain where to go. If you listen quietly, the right thing to do is apparent to you and you move with directness. Fear makes you hurry. Poise lets you pause.

Briefly, these are the points to think about in posture and walking: Keep a straight back; point the sitting bones toward the ground, the top end of the spine toward the sky; walk with rhythm, having the whole body in each step. Do not walk with feet, legs, arms—with many parts.

Let your body show forth the mental qualities of poise which you possess and you will move with confidence and without effort.

This rightness of movement cannot be put on for state occasions only. The directions given here should be used in outdoor walks and in everyday life until they have become your natural style. Then you will be at ease even though you are walking down an aisle, rising to speak, or entering a large platform.

Chapter 17

ON THE PLATFORM

Why does the inexperienced speaker or performer usually anticipate platform work with foreboding? As an audience our demands on him are few. We want to be able to hear and see him. We would like him to be natural. We prefer that his naturalness be agreeable to the eye, free from peculiarities, and that his appearance be pleasing.

No magic formula can be offered that will show you how to meet these requirements. However, this chapter will suggest a few rules which will help you to look at ease until the strangeness of being before the public has worn off and you can completely forget yourself. When you look stiff and uncomfortable an audience suffers with you. What should be your model?

The ideal speaker is as natural as if he were talking to you in his own home. He inspires you with confidence in what he says because of his sincerity and assurance. There is nothing which tempts you to turn away from his message and think of him as a person. Free from mannerisms, his every move is essential and right. You feel easy as you listen to him.

Now let us think through public speaking and find some remedies for the self-consciousness that may grip you when you first have to appear on a platform.

First realize that you are not asked to work at an elevation in order to exalt your person but because you have something of value to give, and you can be seen and heard better from this position than from the floor level of the hall. If you realize this, your interest in your subject will make you glad to be on a platform.

The most prevalent and glaring offense is unnaturalness.

Many who are ordinarily genial will enter a platform looking grim and foreboding. Some will sail on like a ship carefully going into dry dock. A teenager described such a public speaker as having "brought in the body." Much of the beauty of an occasion is lost by the ritualistic, formal actions of those who have not learned to be natural when they are before the public.

The following fundamentals, fully discussed in previous chapters, will help you to get yourself off your hands when you are called upon to appear on a platform.

1. Learn the right way to walk, stand, and sit.
2. Listen with your whole thought focused on the idea—the subject at hand and the group of persons interested in it. With listening, no self-consciousness can creep in.
3. Recognize that ideas are impersonal and contain all that is needed for their expression, and you lose a sense of personal responsibility.
4. Establish unity with the audience through understanding true poise—that feeling of "brother" which places you on the same level, not above nor below those to whom you are speaking.
5. Value your ability, value what you say, and also value the ability of the audience to grasp the meaning.
6. "Be yourself" at all times, free from affectation, presenting your subject with directness and simplicity.

These rules, when they are understood and used, give you freedom almost immediately. Working on the mere techniques of platform procedure often fails because you focus on the *how*. Your full attention needs to be with your subject.

The previous chapter will help you with posture and with walking correctly when entering a platform, but what about the time you are forced to sit on the platform doing nothing, when you feel your face freeze and know you are looking stiff and can't seem to do anything about it. The big thing is to prevent this from happening. Keep interested. Listen attentively when another is speaking. In preparing for this occasion it won't hurt you to take a few minutes before a mirror and see what happens when you let the muscles of the face sag down. Then pick them up with positive constructive thoughts. I can't tell you what these thoughts should be. You will have to work them out for yourself—but do it. You will see that your eyes brighten and open wider, the corners of the mouth lift—not in a synthetic smile but in response to alive thinking. On the platform you dare not waste a moment wondering what kind of an impression you are making or fearing you will not do yourself credit, because your thoughts immediately show in your expression and posture. But unselfish friendly thoughts also show—stay with them.

In your effort for naturalness on the platform, I do not advise following the example of a certain young man who gave talks throughout the United States. He told me that he did everything which most public-speaking teachers taught students not to do. He would take off his coat, his tie, roll up his sleeves, sit on the floor or on the side of the chair leaning over the footlights as he talked. These were not a series of self-indulgent mannerisms, but carefully rehearsed techniques. This man was much in demand as a speaker. Probably because people are tired of the stilted unnatural actions of many of our public performers—so tired that they welcome any escape from their stiff and formal attitude. Even such artificial antics as this person displayed seem a relief.

I recommend informality on the platform, but a controlled naturalness. Habits or idiosyncrasies which your friends and family may enjoy in you become a menace on the platform, for they bring you, instead of your subject, into the picture. Moreover, you may have mannerisms of which you are unaware. Ask one discerning friend to check up on you, and be humble enough to take the criticism you may get. Every action is exaggerated on the platform so you need to be in conscious control of yourself all the time. Shaking the head for emphasis, raising the eyebrows, hooking thumbs in the trouser pockets or vest armholes, adjusting tie—any undue facial or bodily activity —is distracting.

One vivacious young woman who had sparkling black eyes and blinked them when talking, shifting them from side to side, raising her brows, moving her shoulders, and putting on a rather charming performance when she was telling anything, was unable to appear before groups because of self-consciousness. When she learned to drop these distracting mannerisms she was free and now she gives talks and conducts classes before large assemblages with perfect ease.

A lecturer had to reach into his hip pocket for his handkerchief. He unbuttoned his double-breasted coat in order to reach his hip pocket, buttoned it up wrong, after a while discovered his mistake, unbuttoned it, and this time failed to fasten the inside button so that, during the rest of the speech, the point of the under lap of the coat hung down about two inches. Such actions are disconcerting to the audience. Anticipate what you will be doing while on the platform, and work out the procedure so that nothing will interfere with the smoothness of your delivery.

Clothes which "stay put" help to eliminate fidgeting. You cannot afford to be thinking of your clothing while you are before the public, and rightness is the one thing which lets you forget what you are wearing. It is much easier to be natural if you do not feel "dressed up." Often a woman comes on to a platform looking as if she had just stepped out of a beauty shop, every hair in a set place. Somehow the stiffness of her grooming and attire carries into her manner. Overelaborate flowers, jewelry, materials, cut of garments, also interfere. However, respect for your subject should make you careful to give a pleasing effect and then your person can be forgotten.

When a speaker and the one who is to make the introduction
enter a platform, the one who is to introduce the speaker, being
the host, goes first to show his guest the way. When a man is
introducing a woman he should step aside as soon as he enters
and let the woman pass in front of him to her place. The
introducer waits for the speaker to reach his place before sitting
down. The speaker's place is to the right of the introducer. On
a narrow platform, if the speaker and introducer come in so
that the introducer's chair is reached first, he steps beside it,
not in front of it, and waits there for the speaker to pass before
him. Even if the introducer is a woman and the speaker a man,
this is correct. Should the introducer be a woman and the
lecturer a man, the lecturer rises as the introducer rises but
may resume his seat until the formal presentation. Then as
his name is mentioned he rises again and remains standing until
it is his turn to speak.

In sitting on the platform, the legs should not be crossed.
Keep the forward foot flat on the floor. If the feet are stretched
out in front of you so that the soles of the shoes can be seen,
the size of the foot seems enlarged. While you do not want to
make sudden or conspicuous motions, still a statuelike im-
mobility is disconcerting too. If you need to sit for a long time
while another speaks, real listening will give you a relaxed
appearance. You can bring yourself to an erect posture occasionally by pushing down with your elbows. An easy, comfortable position for the hands is to let them rest gently in the
lap, fingers up, one hand resting in the other, or one on the
arm of the chair. Men may prefer to rest them, palms down, on
their legs instead of in their laps. Do not rest hands on both
arms of the chair. Such posture makes you look like the lions
in front of the New York Public Library.

When there is more than one person on the platform there
should be unity of purpose. If one is speaking or reading, the
others should listen. It is not necessary to strike a pose, how-

ever, in order to listen. If you are truly attentive, everything about you shows it and no ritualistic turning, raising of the eyes, or rapt expression, is necessary. Be gracious to the others on the platform with you, considering them, by giving a courteous smile or questioning glance which implies, "I've finished now. Shall we be seated?" Or, when both are about to get up, "Are you ready to rise?" Friendliness between those on the platform spreads to the audience. When another is speaking, guard against looking over papers, making notes, or doing anything which distracts attention from the business which should occupy the center of the stage.

Wait for your audience to become quiet before you start to speak or read, so that none of the message will be lost. During this pause, actually listen yourself. If you begin before there is silence, the clicking of purses, blowing of noses, arranging of wraps often lasts for several minutes. The concert pianist offers a good example of this ability to listen. Usually some moments pass before he and the audience are ready.

A stage producer told of seeing an actor try to remonstrate with an uproarious New Year's Eve audience by saying, "Now of course you realize that we can't go on with the performance unless you co-operate with us." This started them off worse than ever, and the show had to stop because they became unmanageable. But on another occasion an actor completely silenced confusion by calmly listening, not in a reproving way, but as if he expected something to happen. The audience began to listen with him, and he was able to continue the performance.

When standing, a good positive posture helps to give confidence. Let your hands go where gravity takes them. Simply release them. Refuse to let them get in your way. No one else will notice them if they are not in your thought. Avoid all unnecessary movement with the hands and fingers. Hands give you away when you are thinking about yourself. You can make them behave.

When lecturing, if it makes you feel easier to hold something in your hand, you might have a small notebook containing a few notes or quotations which you might want to use in developing your subject. Have everything that you may need for reference in your talk handy and well marked, so that there will be no fumbling and hurried turning of pages. If you refer to notes, do it frankly.

When you start to address a group, your first need is to establish a feeling of oneness with them. Get that friendly sense of being on the same level with the audience. I have the feeling of putting my arm around them and saying, "I'd like you to look at certain ideas with me. They're not mine, but I think they're good and I'm sure you'll like them." With this approach you are right with them and you will not feel isolated. But if you think of yourself as being on the platform in a superior capacity, you will feel separated from your audience because you will have to combat the resistance which they instinctively set up against your attitude of superiority.

Look at the audience. Feel that the occasion includes all of the listeners, even those farthest away or in a position where it is difficult to hear. Then turn wholly to the idea. The constraint which fear and thinking about yourself brings into the voice, vanishes as you become absorbed in your subject, with the result that the voice becomes free and able to go where the thought directs. Remember it is this matter of visualizing the audience, not your vigor, which enables you to be heard. In a hall where the acoustics are poor you may have to remind yourself frequently of the size of the audience, but do it in the pauses, not as you are speaking.

Always speak as if you were addressing one individual. If you try to diffuse your voice out through the hall, it loses its person-to-person appeal. Your voice should sound focused. An experienced after-dinner speaker said that people often came to him following a speech to say that he seemed to be talking just to them. Indeed you are always talking to one—to the listener—no matter which person your eyes rest upon.

A studied eye contact, turning the head from side to side in the effort to include everyone in the audience, is objectionable because it obviously is done for effect. If the speaker is wholly absorbed in his subject, his audience will be also, and will not be concerned with his eye contact.

When a gesture comes to you, make it and let it be a full one. Should you hold it back, it may appear as a little personal wave of the hand. Have all of you in it. As an experiment, try now stretching the arm out, palm up, so that the elbow is not bent. There is a freedom felt and imparted in a full arm gesture. We are too apt to hug ourselves in a self-conscious way, and gesture only with the forearm or hand. Really the movement of the arm is controlled by the muscles of the upper arm and back. If you feel this, you will be less likely to make an awkward half-movement.

In impersonal work such as acting and in some church services no direct contact is made with the audience. We do not want to see a preacher or reader nodding and smiling at friends any more than we like to see an actor come out of his part and bow to the audience, interrupting the action of the play.

In the theater it should be as if there were a fourth wall between the actors and the audience. The public is able to look through that wall and see what is happening but does not want to feel as if the actors know they are being observed. The illusion that the events are actually taking place right now, would be destroyed if the players seemed conscious of their audience.

In a church service the preacher or reader should not be telling the audience things which he knows but which the audience does not. Instead, ideas are coming to him and he sees them *for himself,* and he, like the actor, recognizes that there are others interested in them. For this reason he reads or speaks so that all may hear. Still he does not read *to* them, but rather *with* them.

In reading, the reader and the listeners should have a feeling of oneness, and because of this, the reader does not feel the need of raising his eyes periodically to recognize the audience unless a direct invitation is given. Keeping the eyes on the text helps to avoid the sense of reading *at* anyone. It keeps the reader from catching some person's eye for an instant and distracting the attention of both of them. It avoids the danger of losing the place. Most important of all, it gives a profundity which allows the listeners to get the thought itself, unmixed with a personality. The part the reader plays makes no demand upon him to express anything beyond the ideas he reads. When these ideas are really visualized, their warmth and life hold the attention of the audience better than any eye contact.

The result of constantly looking up and down while reading is apparent in television and movies, where politicians read speeches. Most of them look from script to audience frequently and this movement of the head and eyes is so disconcerting and unnatural that it sometimes causes laughter.

The function of a presiding chairman, or of a lecturer or of one making an introduction is different. He must recognize the audience as soon as he comes onto the platform. If you are performing one of these offices, think of welcoming the people as you walk out.

When possible, go on the platform ahead of time and get used to its feel, to the location of your chair, and the size of the audience. If you are the principal speaker, do not hesitate, before the meeting, to rearrange the platform appointments a bit if they can be made more convenient for you. Where your first introduction to the platform comes at the time of your talk, as is often the case, you can still make minor changes such as adjusting lamp, microphone, or moving a table if need be. An audience enjoys such informality.

A rather inexperienced lecturer was told to stay back of a white tape which had been stretched on the platform to keep him the proper distance from the microphone. A table had been placed about two feet in front of the tape and each time he reached for a book he leaned over the space as if there were a stream of running water between him and the table. How simple it would have been if, after acknowledging the introduction, he had moved the table back where it would have been handy for him.

I find it easier to get the feel of being close to an audience if there is nothing between them and me. If a table or lectern or desk has been placed in the center of the stage, I step beside it, rather than behind it. Standing or sitting behind a desk always gives me the feeling of being a schoolteacher who ensconces herself behind the desk the better to establish her authority.

Of course in this day of amplifiers and broadcasting, there are many times when one must talk from behind a table or lectern. When using a microphone, try to keep a uniform distance away from it. Sometimes when you read and then extemporize, there is the tendency to lean close as you read and draw away as you speak. The resulting unevenness of tone is disturbing to the listeners.

Don't let unexpected happenings throw you off balance. They are sure to occur at times. For example, on one occasion a cat wandered out onto the platform. The lecturer sensed it, turned, picked up the cat, put it on the table and stroked it for a moment saying, "Now pussy, this is a monologue, not a catalogue." Then he handed the cat to an usher who put it out. The audience felt closer to that lecturer as a result of the little break. Had he tried to ignore the presence of the cat, he and the listeners would have been uncomfortably aware of it and unable to give full attention to the subject.

Another interruption that frequently occurs is the seating

of people after the talk has started. If it is a serious subject and you feel that the audience is not with you, stop and wait until you again have their attention. You can sometimes say, "Shall we wait until these people are seated," to explain your pause.

Always define to yourself the purpose of what you are doing. Is it to show that you can give a talk without interruption, no matter what happens, or is it to bring certain ideas to the fore so that everyone can see and feel their value? If it is the latter, refuse to let any circumstance or dilemma defeat this objective.

When reading aloud guard against a preoccupied tone as you turn pages. This blankness of tone is caused by your thought's being distracted from what you are reading to the act of turning the page and finding the new place. Better to have an unusually long pause at the turning of the leaf than to lose the meaning.

In reading the Bible, to bring interest into the tone when announcing the book, think, "What does John say about this subject?" or, "What is in the Psalms about this thought?" When the name of the book is mentioned without thought, it breaks into the continuity of what is read.

After you have finished speaking or reading, turn and walk to your seat. *Do not walk backward.* If you are only one or two steps from your place, you will probably take a side step to your chair and sit down.

Go back to the purpose of everything you do on the platform and let this purpose motivate your gestures, words, phrasing. The more simple and unaffected you make all of your actions, the better.

Do not accept blindly the advice given here, which is culled from my own experience and observation. Every situation calls for a slightly different treatment. If you are sincere and will listen every moment—not to the tones of your voice, but to the ideas which you are expressing—you will know the right thing to do, and will do it naturally and with confidence.

PART IV

EXTEMPORANEOUS SPEAKING

Chapter *18*

LAWS OF EXTEMPORANEOUS SPEAKING

Extemporaneous speaking is a term that covers the major portion of all our speech. Conversing, explaining, selling, teaching —in fact any speech in which the words are not memorized or read—comes under this heading.

Learning to listen is the first step in learning to speak, for listening opens the door to inspiration.

Some shy away from the word *inspiration* because it has been so often used in an emotional way. But here the term is applied to the incoming of ideas, a natural activity which anyone experiences to a greater or lesser degree, before he speaks or acts. True, the word *inspiration* has been applied to that which enabled Robert Browning to write his beautiful and cryptic lines, and this may be one reason you have thought of it as far removed from your life, which usually appears ordinary and humdrum to you. But any and every new and useful idea which comes to your thought is inspiration.

Here are a few simple rules which will help you to talk extemporaneously. They are not elaborate or technical, but they work. An explanation of each rule follows the list.

1. Listen first.
2. Keep on the positive side in your thinking. Guard against negatives which retard your listening and therefore your inspiration.
3. Be willing and expectant when you are going to speak. either in conversation or more formally.
4. When addressing a group, pause before starting.

5. Begin with a good attack on the first words so that listeners are with you from the start.

6. Continue to listen as you talk. Then you will not digress from the subject, will let it inspire your choice of words and phrases, will know how long to stay with each topic, and will know when to stop. Stopping at the right time leaves the listeners still thinking, not surfeited with your theme because you have given too much, nor yet bewildered because they have been left without sufficient information.

Perhaps you remember an occasion when, upon being asked to speak, you could not think of a thing to say but later, possibly as you drove home, idea after idea came to mind, not slowly and painfully, through a figuring-out process, but quickly and without effort. The cause of your difficulty was doubtless that, at the time you were called upon, you allowed your thought to turn inward on yourself, and it became closed and tight, whereas the simple act of turning your thought outward in listening would have opened it to all of the ideas which came to you later. Listening lets the right idea come at the time you need it.

Approach speaking with expectancy, not dread. Confidence comes with a positive attitude of mind. A negative thought such as, "I can't talk on my feet," "What if I rose and couldn't think of anything to say," "These people wouldn't understand my views," will separate you from inspiration. Even *wondering whether* is negative according to *Roget's Thesaurus*. This attitude causes you to teeter back and forth: "I wonder whether I'd better try or not." It brings uncertainty. Do not permit it.

You may think you have nothing to say, but there is always something for you to say in any situation where speech is necessary. Never admit there is not. That is one of the negatives which will stop the flow of thought, whereas expectancy opens the gate wide.

A woman in a speech class insisted that it was impossible for her to speak extemporaneously. In a prepared three-minute assignment, she gave one of the best talks, but when a subject was handed to the class to discuss on the spur of the moment, she did not volunteer, and when called upon said without a moment's hesitation, "I have been listening to all that the others have given with great interest so, of course, I haven't thought of anything to say myself."

She believed that she had been obedient to the instructions given for extemporaneous speaking, and that they had failed her. Had she continued to listen after the others had finished, instead of thinking of this apology, which came like a well-learned speech, the ideas which had to be dragged from her by questions would have come as she was rising to her feet. After this woman saw her mistake, she corrected it, being one of the first to volunteer to talk thereafter, and making worth-while contributions each time. Later she engaged in work in which she was called upon to address large groups. This incident shows what improvement can be made as *self-made* limitations are broken down. Do not be too ready to admit such negatives as: "I have nothing to give." "Ideas don't come to me. Or if they do, they don't amount to much. No one else would like to hear them. And anyway it's too much effort to go through the struggle with myself in order to express them."

If you need to say that you are not informed on a subject, you can do it in a positive natural way, without embarrassment or apology. However, though your mind be a blank when you are called upon to speak, do not hurry to say you have nothing to give. Listen first. You may receive a pleasant surprise at that which springs into your waiting thought, whether long-forgotten experiences or new views. Give them the chance to come.

Always rise as if you want to speak. You gain the confidence of your listeners if you look as if you had something to say. Half the battle is won when the listeners are with you from the start. A self-conscious person will sometimes begin to speak before he rises and will sit down before he has finished.

Be mentally with your subject from the start. If you fail to get inside your subject when speaking to a group, you will sometimes talk for several minutes before you find your stride and gain the attention of the listeners.

Give your first words in a positive tone. Note the effect of this positive attack with the following quotation. First read it, sliding into the words in a thoughtless way; the second time give a good pause before starting and thoughtfully focus on your first words as you read them.

> Every great scientific truth goes through three stages. First, people say it conflicts with the Bible. Next, they say it has been discovered before. Lastly, they say they had always believed it.—LOUIS AGASSIZ

Notice how much more clearly the thought is brought out the second time.

A hazard in extemporaneous speaking is the habit of saying "U-u-u-uh" and "A-a-a-ah" between words and phrases. Often one hooks ideas together with these vague sounds because of his fear of pauses; or because of caution lest he say the wrong thing; or because he lets his attention wander from the subject.

The remedy for this sort of hesitation is to speak a worthwhile thought as it occurs to you and not string it along, trying to think of what should follow. Put your whole thought on what you are saying. Allow definite pauses. Do not fill them with "A-a-a-ah's" or "U-u-u-uh's." In the pauses both you and the listeners can consider what has just been given. Enjoy the pauses.

It was pointed out to a student in a speech class that she used these hesitant sounds many times in one short talk. This uh-ah-ing was so involuntary that she would hardly believe that she did it. By the following week she had overcome the habit. If this is one of your speech faults, you can drop it as quickly.

Express your thoughts spontaneously. Whenever possible avoid committing the words of a speech to memory. There are times when memorizing is demanded of a speaker. See page 217 "To Commit to Memory." The speaker who lets inspiration guide what he says finds many opportunities which the cautious "speech-learner" misses. Unexpected humor, or a completely new approach, may be born to the one who listens for fresh ideas as he goes along. When speeches are learned verbatim, inspiration has small chance. The memorized speech is apt to be like warmed-up hash, not sizzling like a porterhouse steak just out from under the broiler.

In speaking extemporaneously, you will often find yourself as interested in what you are saying as are your auditors. You may think a speech committed to memory is safer—like a raft which will keep you afloat on all occasions. It may be a raft, but it is anchored to the bottom and you are half under most of the time you are on it. True, you will not entirely sink as long as you stay with it. But seldom will you reach the freedom and beauty which is possible, unless you cut away from the learned text and ride the waves of inspiration.

The careless habit of falling into the wording of others is a pitfall to the extemporaneous speaker. It is easy to glimpse an idea and, by quoting another, state only an approximation of what you see. This is especially true of an often heard senti- ment, a cliché, such as "Too full for utterance," "Gay as a lark," "Words fail to express my gratitude." The first time they were said they lived. An idea motivated them. But now they are dead. They have been said so often that you unconsciously use them when you are not mentally alert. They are empty words. The inspiration which brings ideas is vital. It does not offer worn-out phrases for its expression. Know that you have strayed from the idea when you hear yourself falling into an often heard pattern. Stop a moment and listen. Think deeply and clearly about the idea which urged you into speech, and what you say will then take on original, graphic phrasing. Reject all threadbare expressions.

The charm of your speaking lies in telling accurately how things appear to you; they have a special look to you. Do not let it be dulled and weakened by imitation or by drifting lazily into the words and phrases of others. "Be yourself."

Of course, if you need to use better grammar, study grammar so that blunders will not distract attention from what you say. To "be yourself" does not mean to violate the laws of good usage, or to make an effort to be different.

In extemporizing, you must use words as they come, you cannot try to be weighty or grand. If you were not satisfied with your choice of words during a talk, *at another time* work on good synonyms which express your meaning more lucidly. It cannot be done at the moment of action. Only that which is really a part of you can then be used.

A man in a speech class started to use the word "frothy" to describe the present-day thinking. Not feeling it suitable for the occasion, he tried to find one which had more dignity, lost the flow of the ideas and as a result stumbled for a few seconds— something which rarely happened to him. The word "frothy" conveyed his meaning perfectly and should have been used. His reasoning came in and interfered with his accepting the rightness of inspiration.

Avoid apology. Instead of covering an error, apology magnifies it. Many think it is a sign of humility to apologize for what they say and do. It is really a form of egotism, for it turns thought away from the subject matter to the speaker.

A woman who desired to be free when speaking in groups would, in her class talks, put in little side remarks, witty but personal, which would make us think of her instead of what she said. She then wondered why she became self-conscious while speaking. In one talk she observed, "Now I've got myself up on the chandelier and how am I going to get down?" She had worked up to a climax and then had started to flounder. We laughed and saw her hanging there, instead of seeing what she was talking about. She was unable to continue. Pride made her hurry to apologize for a pause. Had she continued to listen for ideas, even though listening entailed an unusually long pause, she would have been able to complete her speech.

Uphold the ideas you give. They are impersonal. Do not limit them by getting in the way, calling attention to yourself, to the manner in which you speak, to your voice, your opinions, your limited knowledge of the subject. You can get in your own way simply by using an apologetic tone.

Equally bad is bragging. Like apology, it turns the listeners' attention to the personality of the speaker.

If you really want to keep people's thought on your subject and away from yourself, there is a way: Be completely engrossed in the ideas. Then your expression of them will form a vivid screen which will completely hide you as a person.

A lecturer, self-forgetful because of his vital interest in his theme, was told after his lecture, "I thought I'd listen to the way you pronounced various words, but I became so occupied with what you said that I was not conscious of your pronunciation." The speaker's technique was hidden by the brilliancy of the ideas. One will always hold attention when he himself is mentally dwelling on his subject. The one who allows his thought to wander—to the audience, to himself, to his technique—loses his listeners.

The method of speaking extemporaneously described in this chapter will not work when the aim is to "put things over." It is of value only as one's motive is to reveal facts, rather than to veil or cover them.

Several of the important forms of extemporaneous speaking have been taken up under separate chapter heads.

Chapter *19*

SHORT TALKS IN OPEN MEETINGS

In business meetings, club meetings, church meetings, et cetera, it is necessary to get the permission of the chairman before you are entitled to speak from the floor. Therefore, you start speaking *as you rise,* to gain immediate attention. Otherwise someone nearer the front, not knowing you are about to say something, may rise and start speaking after you are on your feet, which is embarrassing. It is always harder to make a second start than to speak when the impulse to speak first strikes you. You may gain recognition, either by addressing the chair as "Mr. Chairman," "Madame Chairman," or by starting a sentence as you rise, depending on the nature of the meeting. After the chair has recognized you, it is safe to pause if you do not have the full attention of the audience.

In short talks take up only a few major issues. Keep your attention on each point as you talk, and you will know what to say as well as the right moment to stop. End at a high point, leaving your audience still thinking. Many a good talk has lost its effectiveness because the speaker did not stop at the right time. Some ramble on because they simply do not know how to close. Follow Sir Winston Churchill's advice, "Say what you have to say, and when you come to the end of a grammatical sentence, sit down." Others talk too long because they enjoy talking. One student complained, "Inspiration told me to sit down but I didn't want to." You cannot tell all you know in three minutes or less. One or two key points, clearly stated, are more potent than a dozen, hurriedly touched upon. James

Russell Lowell warned about "having too much to say, so that words, hurrying to escape, bear down and trample out the life of each other."

To keep continuity in your talk, stay with the idea. This will prevent jumping from one subject to another and back to the first. Every sentence, every word, every pause, needs to be relevant. Self-indulgence makes you wander afield to tell interesting things which do not directly apply to the subject at hand, and often the destination is never reached. Success as a speaker depends upon arriving.

A strong first sentence should open your talk. This may be planned before you rise, and it will serve to start the flow of ideas. But you lose in power if you try to anticipate while you are talking, for it takes your thought away from what you are saying at the moment. The immediate idea, if seen distinctly and presented distinctly, leads naturally to the next sequence. If the present thought is neglected you will not be ready for the new one. In speaking, as in reading, the law is one thing at a time.

Be with the idea as you present it. No amount of beautiful diction or studied poise can be substituted for this focus.

Chapter *20*

TO CONDUCT A GROUP
MEETING—A CONFERENCE

In conducting group meetings of any nature, the first step is to ask yourself, "What is the purpose of this meeting?" Then listen until you get inspiration about it. Unless you know what you are aiming for, how can you arrive? Too often a chairman starts with, "How did Dudley do it last year?" and then proceeds to limit himself and the group by imitating an outdated occasion.

Write down the things that occur to you about the meeting, regardless of order. Later you can arrange them under general headings, as:

1. Notifying those who will attend.
2. Preparation of hall.
3. Notifying those who will help in the preparation.
4. Arranging the order of business.

Clearly visualize each part of your meeting. Arrange the seating so that no one faces glaring light. Provide good lighting for those who need it. See that the speaker or performer can be seen.

Definite directions prevent mistakes. Is there someone to open the hall, arrange the seats, platform, amplifier, watch the temperature of the room?

For the meeting itself, you, as chairman, will have a smoother time if you are familiar with *Robert's Rules of Order*. Make an itemized program of business to be transacted. It is up to you to keep control and guide the procedure toward the purpose. In discussion, by careful listening and a positive attitude and tone, you can clarify faltering statements made from the floor, impersonalize arguments, see that both sides of a question have an equal chance to be heard, and not allow parliamentary procedure to be cumbersome.

Should self-consciousness bother you when presiding, there is a sure remedy. Be so interested in the idea back of the meeting that you focus the full thought of others on this idea. The result will be that you cannot be thinking of yourself, and no more can they.

The purpose of the meeting, or of the business session portion of the meeting, may be to clarify obscure propositions which are to be voted on in a forthcoming election. But often the main speaker, who has probably donated his service, is kept waiting while trite business or dull announcements or jokes nibble away the time. An alert chairman will not permit this to happen.

A group gathered to hear a renowned traveler may have the edge taken off their expectancy by a chairman who feels called upon to drag all of his fellow workers into the limelight, in an attempt to show how modest he is, thus losing sight of the occasion's underlying purpose. The meeting becomes cluttered with personality-padding and bouquet-throwing while the speaker sits there—an outsider in these "old home" demonstrations, when he should be the center of attention.

"Lack of time" is the cry of the people. Consider this fact and in conducting your meeting let every step be relevant— nothing done merely because you think it "the thing to do." Do not waste words with unimportant flourishes. Present the information, transact the business, introduce the speaker as directly as possible, leaving the personal, amusing, or social features for the last.

Conferences

The conference, the gathering together of a group with a common interest for the purpose of discussion, consultation, the pooling of information, or for training, is extremely popular today, particularly in the business world. The conference has this democratic aim: to give each person a chance to express his feelings and to participate in the forming of the policies under which he acts. However, its advantage is curtailed by the inability and unwillingness of persons to express themselves before a group. If the opportunity for mutual understanding and the pooling of valuable knowledge which the conference offers is not realized and appreciated by those taking part, the leader may find himself with a dead weight on his hands. He must know how to bring the group to life, how to encourage participation, how to keep the talk relevant to the subject at hand, how to time the discussion, and how to summarize and point up what has been covered so that the members of the group know exactly what they have accomplished.

Should you have charge of a conference, start by defining its purpose. Then quietly listen and write down the ideas which occur to you about the subject to be covered; note provocative questions to stimulate discussion. Naturally such questions should not be phrased so that they can be answered by Yes or No.

Do all you can to create an informal, friendly atmosphere, because it helps people to express themselves. Many conferences take place around a large table. When this is not practical, use any irregular seating arrangement which makes it easy for the members to talk together. If you stand or sit in front of the group, questions and comments are automatically addressed to you. This is the wrong procedure in a conference. Don't let the others turn to you to answer their questions, to judge the merit of an opinion, or to express approval or disapproval. Turn the questions over to the group. You can even turn a general question to a particular person who you think can answer the query. Parliamentary procedure is ignored in a conference unless it is necessary to vote on an issue.

Start with a clear statement of the subject and its relation to the group. Then ask a question which will open the discussion. Or where no explanation is necessary, you may start with the question. Wait for an answer. Put the meeting in the hands of the group; don't feel it is your responsibility. If you are self-conscious, you may not be able to weather the long pause which frequently occurs when a vital issue is presented to a group, and will be inclined to answer for them or to ask another question. Remember that probably they did not start listening as soon as you presented the question. It may take them a few moments to realize that you are giving them the floor, so do not be afraid to wait. I understand that in Quaker group meetings they sometimes have silence for five minutes at a stretch, and occasionally for an hour. Do some listening to the idea yourself and you will be better able to appraise the contributions of others. Do not allow yourself to be anxious or resentful because there is not a ready response. This negativity blocks the very response you want. Should you feel that you did not state the question clearly the first time, you might rephrase it to be sure the group understands it.

Once the talking begins, you must ever be alert to keep it relevant. Hold a firm rein on it and turn it back quickly and positively if it starts to digress. One leader who was to conduct a group regularly for a year, allowed them to wander for about half an hour at their first meeting without rebuke. Then he said, "Now you see what happens if we do not keep to the subject. I'm sure you will understand if I insist that we stay with one point at a time." From then on, with the full co-operation of the rest of the group, he resolutely limited all discussion to the point at hand with the result that the business was covered more effectively and in a much shorter time than ever before.

Encourage people to think aloud in a conference. A speech is not the need. In fact it is not desirable. You want an alert pooling of information and opinion which will open out the thought of all the members to the subject at hand and to an agreement about it. One highly paid official used to attend conferences and remain perfectly quiet until the subject had been thoroughly talked over. Then in well chosen words he would state the conclusion which the efforts of all had brought to light. At a surface view it would look as if he were a deep thinker and always gave the substantial contribution which clinched the conference, whereas actually he contributed little, merely coming in at the kill to claim the victory. This is not the purpose of the conference. It would never reach its objective if everyone proceeded in this fashion.

Do not let anyone talk too long or have the floor too often. Certain people have to be definitely interrupted for the sake of the discussion, so that all may participate. The meeting is vital only when everyone is thinking about the idea presented and eager to see it clarified, alert and ready to contribute—not when they sit lethargically waiting for ideas to be spoon-fed to them.

Sometimes one who is well-informed or vitally interested will answer all the questions you raise. But questions are presented for the purpose of stimulating thought, not to obtain a ready answer. You may find it advisable to explain to such a person, outside of the meeting, that it is better to let the group think for a few moments and give some of the answers rather than for him to speak so often. He will readily understand your reason for this request. In a business lecture, a man remarked that he was afraid he talked too much in conferences, but that there were points which he knew needed to be brought up while the group were together. Because their leader was not alert he found himself talking more than he should. I suggested that he might ask questions, even though he knew the answers, in order to promote discussion and bring out pertinent information in an impersonal way.

Encourage the shy person by asking him a question which is easily answered, but not one which can be answered by a monosyllable or he will take that way out. Usually all he needs is to get started.

I have seen a man who is very deliberate, start to speak two or three times, but before he got the words out a quick person jumped in and took the floor. You can make an opening for the deliberate speaker by asking what he wanted to say.

Ask the one who looks bored a challenging question. Clarify for the one who does not express himself well, so that the group will not lose interest. You might say, "Did you mean this, Mr. Smith . . . ?" If you have misinterpreted him, your statement usually will help him to say what he does mean.

If two or three are talking in an aside, bring them into the main group by asking them to speak louder so that all can hear what they are saying.

Insist that those who really know, contribute by asking them questions which will draw out their knowledge. Other members of the conference appreciate gaining their information. This sharing of experience makes a conference worth while. It is usually difficult to attain and depends largely upon your ability as a leader to keep the glib talker within bounds in a tactful way, and to encourage the well-informed persons to contribute.

Close a meeting as soon as it has reached its objective. Do not drag it out because more time was allotted to it. Should the group not finish the discussion, it is better to arrange for another conference than to overrun your time. Summarize your points even when the meeting is adjourned to another time, so that the group leaves with a clear-cut understanding of what has been accomplished.

If you are to be a competent chairman you must be well-versed in the subject of the conference and also an alert, discriminating listener, or it will be difficult for you to grasp the points which have been made and to summarize and clarify them at the end. You may find it helpful to jot down the main

points as they are given. If a conference is to reach its objective
—that is, if the group is to come to a joint understanding, conclusion, or decision about certain matters—you must be able to
make clear to them where they have arrived and what is the next
step to be taken.

Be brief, natural, and to the point.

Chapter 21

CONVERSATION

In this fast-moving age of noisy airplanes, radio, and television, there seems to be little time or opportunity for real conversation. We scarcely know what it is. *Crabb's English Synonyms* defines it in part as "the rational employment of social beings, who seek by an interchange of ideas to purify the feelings and improve the understanding." Certainly a worthy employment and one which sounds so inevitably right that you would think we would make every effort to bring it into our experience. But we do not understand conversation. We confuse it with talking.

Funk and Wagnall's Dictionary points out under the definition of *conversation* that it is different from *talking* in that "talk may be wholly one-sided. Many brilliant talkers have been incapable of conversation." You doubtless know several. They dominate any group with their wit and intellect, but while they may amuse and entertain and even instruct, they leave the many silent members of the group with a frustrated sense of their own inadequacy.

A good conversationalist does not do this. He not only speaks well, but stimulates others to talk also, drawing them out by means of provocative questions or comments, and enriching the discussion by bringing in the varied experiences and understanding of those in the group. With sincerity and true interest in the subject under consideration he firmly insists that others enter into the talk. Each individual leaves a group where this mutual expression is free and spontaneous, with the contented glow which comes from having been an active participant.

Certain times and places encourage this freedom. Have you

ever been with a congenial group seated around a large fire when a subject vital to the group was launched? In such a situation you were no doubt able to enter into what was said, to contribute, to enjoy what others gave, to get that feeling of "togetherness" which comes as a group watches an idea unfold. The idea seems to open itself, sometimes one, sometimes another commenting. The unobtrusive murmur of the fire with an occasional sharp crack occupies the pauses so you are not afraid of them, and do not hurry to fill them with words. There is no self-consciousness. Your eyes are on the fire but your mind is on the idea. There is a clarity of vision which comes with this impersonal outlook.

Is this ideal conversation dependent upon a waning fire and informal surroundings? It need not be. You can enjoy such enriching conversation often if you understand what brings about good talk.

Listening is the starting point. To the calm and receptive mind come topics suitable for the occasion and the group. Value these ideas and you will present them in a way that causes others to appreciate them. Listen with interest to what others contribute—not with an obvious focus on the person, which is sometimes disconcerting, but with a mental focus on the idea. Be as unafraid of pauses as you were when sitting before the fire. You must have moments of silence to allow the words of each speaker to crystallize and to feel the next step in the unfoldment of the idea. Without pauses there will be frequent repetition and digression from the subject. One speaker's jumping in the minute another stops, is likely to indicate that he was thinking of what he would say as soon as he got a chance and had separated himself from the discussion as a whole. When this happens, conversation is apt to get personal and argumentative. Impersonal conversation does not mean thoughtless acquiescence to whatever is said, but it does preclude trying to put over pet theories. You are reaching for the truth, no matter who voices it, not trying to prove that you know all the answers.

Interest in people, in situations, and in ideas causes you to observe and read; this, in turn, provides you with a storehouse of information to draw upon when you talk. Your own life with its varied activities offers material which is interesting enough to share with others if told freshly and aptly.

Give importance to what you say. Many a useful idea has been hidden in cluttered expression, lost in a vague or apologetic tone, or depreciated by an uncertain laugh.

The habit of sliding into sentences is as damaging in conversation as it is in public speaking. If people do not listen to you when you are in a group, try a good attack on your first words and you will find people begin to pay attention to what you say.

Another prevalent habit when speaking is to let the voice trail off toward the end of a sentence, even leave it unfinished if you think the listener has already grasped your meaning. *Stay with the idea mentally until you have finished speaking.* Support it. Do not go off to what you want to say next. Remember that the thought is to the speaker what the paint is to the artist. Carry through to the end mentally.

If the subject under discussion is unfamiliar, reaching out for more knowledge of it will bring intelligent questions to mind. Ask them, for they stimulate the conversation. If you think, "I don't know anything about this subject," "I have so little general information," "I don't get time to keep up with my reading," and consequently withdraw mentally, your disinterest and self-centered thought dampens the general tone of the group and you become a definite liability.

Do not try to talk about something you do not understand. It is no sin to be unfamiliar with subjects, particularly in this day of specialization. As Will Rogers said, "We are all ignorant. We are just ignorant about different things." The truly educated make no boast of knowing everything, and unhesitatingly admit their ignorance.

Needless to say, bragging is tiresome; and *numerous personal opinions* spoil a conversation. "*I* always think that people should . . ." "If *I* were you, . . ." Conversation that is about ideas has general interest, but the personal, unless it brings out a point in opening up a subject, usually does not encourage others to participate. Guard against becoming too personal. Especially does the one who talks easily, err in this direction.

A hostess who is impressed with the responsibility of getting her guests to talk defeats her purpose if she asks a question and then, instead of listening to the answer, turns to another and asks another question. It takes at least two for a conversation, one to give and one to receive. She must not leave the speaker isolated with no one listening to him. If she will really listen to the reply to her first question she may start a lively discussion into which others will soon join (presuming the introduced subject to be an interesting one). She may then turn her attention to unoccupied guests.

A loquacious person is often tempted to do all the talking for those close to him, who do not have his readiness of tongue. While a married couple were calling on friends, the man, who had been through recent adventures of great interest, was not given the opportunity to open his mouth. His wife told in detail all that had befallen him, and he sat there as helpless as a baby who has not yet learned to talk. Give the quiet ones a chance! Even though you feel that they may not do justice to what they tell, let them relate their own experiences. Encourage them by listening, not interrupting or interpolating.

To monopolize is the mark of a poor conversationalist. But it is equally as bad to refuse to participate. Contrary to general opinion, holding back is as unnecessary as taking over. One who contributes nothing may think he is being a good listener. He may appear calm and poised and may not interrupt when you are speaking, but he volunteers little and seldom shows his interest by asking a question. What might become a lively discussion then drops from its flight and, after a few faint flutters, gives up the ghost. The active phase of listening is not there; it is the quiet, alert appreciation and interest in others which stimulates the giver and receiver alike.

Another who contributes little is the one who has no confidence in himself. Ideas come to him but he thinks more of what people think of him than he does of the ideas. Could he but realize that ideas have their own motor power, he would know that he can go ahead and express them with assurance. Instead he sits back and criticizes mentally the one who does express himself. This critical attitude invariably goes with repression.

The one who thinks he has no ideas is, of course, the one who has not learned to listen. A woman who had always thought this about herself, after attending two lessons in our studio, went to a dinner party and found she could take part in the conversation more easily than she ever had in her life. She began to listen with interest to those speaking to her. This kept her thought turned outward away from herself and on the subject at hand. Spontaneously she was able to give pertinent incidents from her own experience and to ask intelligent questions. She was amazed to hear herself conversing without fear or self-consciousness.

Interrupting, as a habit, is destructive to conversation. One of your excuses for doing this may be, "Why, if I didn't interrupt, no one else would get a chance to say anything. He talks all the time!" Continuous talking often comes from nervousness. Listening attentively to such a talker sometimes awakens him to what he is doing, and will cause him either to stop in confusion or to give more careful heed to what he is saying. If listening does not quiet him, you may have to interrupt. But try listening before adopting this easier but less constructive silencer.

In a group of people of broad and varied experience, one woman monopolized the conversation, airing her limited and personal views without pause. Finally the host, in a firm voice, started another subject, and as she rattled on, he continued in a slightly raised voice until she had to stop. It was a premeditated and effective procedure. When, later, she started again, he did the same thing and this time succeeded in stopping the continuous flow.

When interruption is necessary, let it be positive and apparent.

Another excuse often given for interrupting is, "What he says isn't worth listening to." Again, constructive listening for ideas will occasionally cause the speaker to pay more attention to what he says. Sometimes a question about some constructive subject will change the trend of thought.

Then a third excuse for interrupting: "I know ahead of time just what he is going to say, but it takes him so long to get it out that I go ahead and finish it for him." We sometimes think we can anticipate another's thoughts when we cannot. Perhaps he has an individual way of expressing his idea which would be profitable to hear. Give him the chance to do it. Discipline yourself to listen quietly. Your attention encourages him and relieves you of the strain which comes with impatience. Although you know what someone is about to say long before he says it, when you make yourself stay with him mentally, the subject unfolds to you with unbelievable clarity, not only from what he says, but from the idea itself. As you can enjoy a musical classic an endless number of times, so you may be enriched by a repeated idea. You get the feel of it rather than merely seeing it intellectually. Those who get a surface view quickly, seldom stay with an idea long enough to experience all that an idea contains.

This feel of ideas does not come through words alone. A young woman of modest station married a prominent government official. She discovered that when they entertained foreigners whose language she did not know, she could, if she were not self-conscious, and if she listened carefully, get the sense of what they were saying and could give them the feeling that she took part in their conversation. Not only this, but through her ability to forget herself, and through her poise, feeling neither inferior nor superior to those about her, she was able to converse with many great men, from Justices of the Supreme Court to foreign diplomats, as if they were her own close friends.

This feeling of unity exists in any good conversation. You can always learn something. You can always give something. Refuse to be bored. Listen and enter in and you can be an interesting and interested conversationalist.

The late Harvard Professor, Charles Townsend Copeland, once invited some of his favorite students to his chambers. A sophomore asked, "How does one go about learning the fine art of conversation?" The professor lifted an admonishing finger and said, "Listen, my boy." After a moment's silence, the student said, "Well, I'm listening." Copey said, "That's all there is to it."—BENNETT CERF, in *The Saturday Review*. From June, 1953, *The Reader's Digest*, Courtesy of *The Reader's Digest*.

Some world-wise people were talking about a famous man who has slipped out of popularity.

"He has forgotten how to listen," was the verdict.

It seems to me that everyone can take a tip from this. Of all social graces, the art of listening is probably the most profitable, and it is one of the least used. Learning how to listen while another talks is not as easy as you may believe. A really expert listener is not one of the too eager, the go-on-tell-more variety, and an expert listener is certainly not a *yesser*. Too often we confuse the art of listening with the craft of *yessing*.

A good listener is a quiet, casual listener, one who shows unobtrusively that his mind is alert, appreciative, understanding.

The art requires practice. It's worth it.—PRINCESS ALEXANDRA KROPOTKIN, in *Liberty Magazine*

In America conversation is a game played with rules differing from England's. It is not tennis, in which you return the other fellow's service, but golf, in which you go on hitting your own ball. It might be defined as a tyranny of anecdote tempered by interruption.—RAYMOND MORTIMER, From *The Reader's Digest*, June, 1949, p. 120. Courtesy of *The Reader's Digest*.

One told funny stories, one danced and one sang,
One played the piano until the roof rang.
One did imitations, one turned acrobatic,
And one entertained with tales epigrammatic.
But I, without talent to shine or amuse,
Was shortly the center, the focus, the fuse,
Since—far more important than all those who glistened—
I was the one guest who stopped, looked and listened.
—HARRY LAZARUS, *Party People*. Copyright, 1953, by The Curtis Publishing Company. Courtesy of the author.

Chapter 22

SELLING

One important form of extemporaneous speaking is selling. The salesman is constantly talking to clients and if he is to succeed his conversation needs to be inspired.

Think through the mental approach to selling. Say you are considering undertaking the sale of a certain article or idea. First you investigate it to see if it sells itself to you. This does not mean that you would necessarily want it yourself, but unless you see its merits you cannot hope to make others see them.

A woman working in a store which handled cheap things found herself thinking, "Who would ever use these curtains?" Then she recognized that the garish curtains would please some people. As many prefer a swing record to a Beethoven symphony, so these curtains would be the preference of certain types of persons. After she had impersonalized her viewpoint of the various products in her department, she was able to show and sell them successfully.

Another woman who worked in a large high-class furniture store noticed that she always sold the articles she liked much more quickly than the others. This is too personal a method for good selling. See the uses of what you sell in an impersonal way, *not in the light of your own needs*. Then as you see the wants of your customer, you will know what you have that is suitable for him.

After you are convinced of the usefulness of what you contemplate selling, apply the three steps of expression: Listen, value, express.

Your most useful "hunches" come as you listen: ways to learn more about your product, ways to get in touch with those who might want it. Value them. Then act—communicate with your prospective client. If you reach him through personal contacts, make plenty of them—not just perfunctory calls, but inspired ones. Value your product, value your ability to present it, value your client's ability to appreciate it, and follow through with your project. Do not turn away from the idea you are selling and let discouragement come in.

It is usually wise to make an appointment before calling, so that you can expect a few minutes of undivided attention. Have too much respect for what you sell and for yourself to talk about it when the client is busy.

Before calling on a client, redefine to yourself what you are selling. Be full of it, so that you will not take on his opinion of it. When you actually meet him, keep on the positive side in your own thought, for a negative outlook will separate you from the inspiration which you need to direct your approach. Be expectant, not apprehensive. Have the poise which eliminates the feeling of either inferiority or superiority.

Selling should never influence another to take something he does not want. Its function is to show an idea so distinctly that those who have use for it will want it.

A machine-gun fire of high-pressure salesmanship on the prospective buyer frightens him. What would you do if you were fired at? Probably build a defense. So does the customer who has a line of talk aimed at him. He gets behind his defense and even if he wanted the article or idea he would be unable to see it because he had taken refuge back of a wall of caution. If you do bag him with this pressure method, he may have given in against his better judgment. Afterwards, when he can think without interference, he will either return the article or resolve never to give you another opportunity.

Instead of using the machine-gun method you should turn the searchlight of clear visualization upon the article, so that he may see it plainly. Your attitude should imply, "Will you consider this idea with me? I am not going to try to influence you but I would like you to see it. When you know just what this is, you can feel free to take it or leave it." You and he have unity of purpose. He has no need to hide out when you treat him in this way, and as a consequence he is able to make an independent decision.

The head of an insurance company, keen and dynamic, changed his whole method with his sales staff as a result of learning this power of listening. One of his salesmen had found the advocated high-pressure method very difficult; he was unhappy in his business relations; but after the change of policy he could use the listening idea and really enjoy selling.

A salesman who sold many kinds of building material, through learning to listen more and to talk less, increased the number of his sales. Most of the contractors were familiar with what he sold, and his quietness gave them a chance to make up their mind without outside pressure. They worked together on the transaction, instead of sparring at arm's length.

Another man, when he first tried to use listening in his selling, found that his business lagged. Through questioning I discovered that he was not listening alertly. He thought listening in selling meant an easygoing manner instead of an eager, vital attitude. Being by disposition indolent, he had slumped into a negative method. Before entering the office of a prospective buyer he neglected to focus his whole thought on what he sold, —an essential if he was to describe the product clearly. He had to learn that listening really took more alertness than talking at random. When he really listened, his sales increased.

Another man who was a successful salesman was asked in a salesmanship course how he started with a customer. He said that he went in, greeted his customer, and then listened for a lead. "You'd know that would be his approach. Look at his ears!" exclaimed the teacher. They were large and slightly protruding. This method was highly commended. However, you will find that listening is not dependent on the size of your ears, but on your ability to turn thought outward, away from self, in service to the ideas you are selling.

Expect a sale to be made without delay. When you listen for the best way to proceed, inspiration directs whom you contact, the time, what you say, and the sale is made when the buyer sees the idea clearly enough to know that he wants it. The sale is the natural culmination of the transaction and is included in the idea.

Always be prepared to take the order as soon as a decision is reached. Not only does alertness help you but it is a kindness to the client for it relieves him from that uncomfortable uncertainty which often grips the one trying to settle a course of action—especially if the decision involves a considerable amount of money.

Should you have to reopen the sale, it must be a totally new transaction, not a repetition. It is another day; treat it as a different situation entirely.

Never imitate another's way of selling. You may learn from another but do not imitate him. Your method must be developed individually according to your own talents. It is imperative to be yourself in order to do your best work.

A bond salesman became a member of a new, active concern. Many salesmanship meetings were held in which successful businessmen addressed the salesmen. One speaker advised telling the prospect a funny story in order to win him through a good laugh. That procedure is fine if it is natural to you, but it would not do for this particular man, who was deliberate and serious by nature. His firm used a visual machine, showing charts to illustrate its selling points. Certain of the executives regarded it as infallible; but this man knew that charts could not be used profitably in every case as they completely bewilder some people. Before going in to see a client he would have an argument with himself as to whether he should take the machine or not. His uncertainty made his work drudgery. Confused by the many methods presented, he came for some private instruction on selling.

When asked why he had quit his remunerative business as a bond salesman to take up this work, all the borrowed speeches disappeared. His tone became sure and earnest. "I have been studying stocks and bonds many years. I took courses on them at Columbia University and I understand them thoroughly. Selling them has made me a good income. When this new idea was presented, which is along the same line, I went back to Chicago and investigated the company. It is absolutely sound. I have invested in it myself and so has my wife."

Here was his natural selling talk. It convinced. There was sincerity in it—also authority. When this fact was pointed out to him he was immediately relieved. He saw that what he needed to do was simply to "be himself" when he was selling; also that if he were wide-awake he would be guided by the conversation whether to use the visual machine or not. He said that the labor vanished from his work with this approach and he did so well that he was made district manager of a new territory.

Sales talks should be extemporaneous. A glaring example of memorized sales patter is that of the small boy who comes to your door to sell you a woman's magazine. He has been taught a set speech about what his magazine contains, and although you hear every word as he rattles it off, you cannot grasp what he says, because it means nothing to him. Learned sales speeches are ineffectual. The customer needs only to come in with an unusual question to put the salesman completely off his routine. You should be well informed about what you sell, even to thinking of good adjectives and phrases to describe it, but let them spring spontaneously into use as the occasion demands.

Memorized speeches often make one talk longer than is necessary. He is more concerned with his speech than with his customer's state of mind, and does not discern when he has made the sale.

Make a special point not to talk too much. Give your client a chance to think. As in short speeches, let inspiration tell you when to stop talking. Also do not take his time by talking after a sale is made.

When selling in a store avoid meeting your customer with courteous indifference. Lack of interest separates you from him and you naturally are unable to comprehend his needs. Indifference is fatal to good selling. However, indifference must not be confused with the helpful "take-it-or-leave-it" attitude which leaves the buyer free to make his own decisions.

"Comparisons are odorous" in selling. Your business is to enable the client to see the virtues of what you are selling, not to run down another's wares. As you see the value of your own article or idea, it helps another to appreciate it, but if you bring up the inferiority of some other article, it does not necessarily make him see the good points of yours. It may turn his attention away from your product so that you defeat your purpose, which was to have him see your merchandise distinctly enough to want it.

To sell your own ability seems more difficult than to sell some article. When seeking employment or selling your services, you may find it not so easy to give an impersonal appraisal of yourself as of something which is separate from you. Too often you do not look at yourself dispassionately enough to see exactly what you have to offer. You mark yourself down, because you look away from the ideas you express, and are afraid someone will think you are conceited if you state your talents at face value. Remember that the one who considers employing you is not interested in your modesty but in your ability. You should be as kind to yourself as you would be to your best friend. Think of the way you would present him, and you may be helped in selling yourself convincingly. Think of what you have, not of what you lack.

Watch that you do not speak with a rising inflection. A rising inflection depreciates a statement. For example, to say, "My name is John Smith," sliding the voice up on the word *Smith,* makes it sound as if you thought, "Not that he amounts to anything" or "Not that you are interested." State your name positively. "My name is John Smith (period)." Value it as you say it. Then others will value what it stands for. You are not trying to please. You are not fearing criticism. Give yourself a chance to be seen for what you are, and you will sell yourself without pushing or apologizing. Impersonalize the transaction and you will do it effectively.

Chapter *23*

INTRODUCTIONS—
ANNOUNCEMENTS

Here is an audience and a speaker. Why have an introducer?

Have you ever noticed how animals sniff suspiciously at an outsider who appears in their midst? There is a small amount of the same tendency in the best of us. We may not know the speaker, and we unconsciously take on a skeptical attitude toward him and what he may say. Now the introducer can break down that feeling and bring the audience and the speaker together. Not only should he interest the audience in what the speaker is to say, but he should also interest the speaker in his audience and arouse in him a fresh appreciation of his subject.

The introducer is the host so he should express hospitality, graciousness, interest in the guests. If you are an introducer, guard against a heavy sense of responsibility; be spontaneous and expectant, with no thought of self or of the impression you are making.

In the chapter "On the Platform" you will find suggestions about entering the platform and accepted seating arrangements for introducer and speaker.

An introduction should be as short as possible and still fulfill its purpose. In it you may welcome the visitors; also, if the occasion warrants, touch on the subject of the speech by telling some experience which shows its practical value. This reference may give the alert speaker a springboard from which to start his talk. Perhaps you will also wish to tell of the lecturer's qualifications—why he has been asked to talk to this group. Avoid turning the audience to yourself by apology, or by "stealing the spotlight." Also, do not draw attention to the speaker

himself, for you give him the added task of redirecting the
attention of his audience away from his personality to his theme.

As in other talks, extemporaneous wording is preferable.
Sometimes it is required that the introduction be written and
committed to memory. When this is necessary, define to yourself the nature of the event, reach out for the need of this
particular occasion, and write as if you were speaking spontaneously. The laws for extemporaneous speaking apply likewise to
writing. Let there be no imitation of former introductions, no
hackneyed phrases; keep your words alive instead of dull or
remote. A host is friendly.

Should you have difficulty in memorizing, the chapter "To
Commit to Memory" on page 217 will be helpful.

Say each thing simply. Do not orate or talk with an accumulative tone, such as politicians use as they add fact upon fact, or
M.C.'s as they let the voice soar at the end of each phrase. A
woman introducing several speakers at a dinner spoke in this
way:

We are very/for-tunate/in having/with us/today a ma-an of

much experience/and he has very kindly consented/to tell

us some of his adventures/in the South ⌐Seas.

You heave a sigh of relief when such an introduction is over,
for this suspended tone leaves you dangling until the end—an
uncomfortable position to be in. Again I urge—be natural.

It is not wise to mention the name of the speaker until the
formal presentation, as it is likely to bring applause and
interrupt the introduction. It also causes the lecturer to rise in
response to his name and stand, to no purpose, while the introduction is being completed. This is unfortunate for the attention moves to the speaker and away from what is being said. A
good introduction can be a real contribution toward bringing
the speaker and audience together.

The formal presentation is the high point. *Continue to face the audience as you speak his name:* "Ladies and gentlemen, I present to you *Mr. <u>William</u> <u>Winston</u>.*" Then turn to him, "Mr. Winston." As you say this really look at him as if he were a friend whose address you keenly anticipate. Be sure that everyone present hears the name of the one being introduced. After he has risen, sit down, or turn and walk to your seat, as the case may be. Do not back to your chair. When introductions are given as an assignment in class it seems almost impossible to get an introducer to continue to look at the audience as he gives the name of the speaker. He will invariably turn to the speaker. The audience are the ones who need to hear the name.

During the address, really listen. In case you sit on a platform, it is unnecessary to look like a statue, scarcely blinking. Such unnaturalness makes the audience feel uncomfortable. The introducer should feel easy and relaxed, but, of course he will not make unnecessary movements as movements seem exaggerated from the platform. On occasion the introducer may leave the platform after his introduction, returning the moment the speech is finished.

At the conclusion of an address, if you again take charge of the meeting, thank the speaker graciously, and do not allow him to sit down with no recognition of his contribution. The acknowledgment, however, should be short and impersonal, not an effort to sum up what has been said. In case the meeting ends with the conclusion of a lecture, turn to the speaker immediately, shake hands with him, and show appreciation. Accompany him off the platform and perform any slight courtesy, such as picking up his brief case or helping him with his coat. Be as thoughtful as to a guest in your own home.

Announcements

Think how many announcements are given daily—in business firms, in schools, in clubs, in organizations of every sort.

And observe how little of the information given in this way is really grasped by those hearing it. Unless the one giving the announcement knows how to command attention, how to speak with inspiration, how to visualize well, how to move people to action, the announcement has little value.

How can announcements be made more effective?

Of course the general instructions for reading and speaking given in this book will help. However, a few special rules may be useful to the one who has this function to perform.

1. *Be sure you can be heard.* People will not strain their ears, as a rule, to hear an announcement given in an inarticulate way. They are not yet interested so they do not bother to listen. To break down this attitude, take in the whole group mentally and intend to be heard.

2. *State what you are announcing.* Usually you gain a certain amount of interest by announcing your subject at the beginning. For example, you might start with, "The season tickets for the Light Opera Summer Series are going on sale this week." Warning: Do not give the "vital statistics" at this time. The people are not interested yet and you may easily lose their attention if you go into details of time and place at this point.

3. *Kindle interest.* The ways in which you would kindle interest vary according to the group you are addressing. If telling a men's group about the Light Opera Series you might emphasize the gorgeous girls or the comedians in the cast; to a group of women, the music and excellent costuming. Announced in a movie studio, you would perhaps speak of the producer or of the staging and scenery. Visualize your group and listen for the best way to arouse their interest. Again I would advise extemporizing although you can have notes so that you will not miss any important points.

4. *After you have their interest, give the vital statistics.* Tell them clearly where the event is to be held, on what date, how much it will cost. Don't be satisfied with merely stating the facts. When you mention the location, give some landmark which will place it for them: "The operas will be given at the Philharmonic Auditorium, Fifth and Olive Streets—diagonally across from the Biltmore Hotel. It's handy to good places to eat and the best parking facilities in the city—five floors of the Biltmore Garage and then, right across the street, the Municipal Garage." If the place is difficult to find, you will build up your attendance by helping your listeners to visualize exactly how to reach the place and where they can park. People avoid uncertainty. Take the time to impress on their thought the important points for them to know—in this case, when the event starts, how long it runs, how much it costs.

5. *Call for action.* Give them something to do. "I will take your order for tickets. There are only a limited number of seats available because the holders of season tickets keep them year after year." Something which will move them to action *now*.

Chapter *24*

LONG TALKS

Long talks, such as lectures, sermons, reports, assembled information, ordinarily require preparation of the material to be used. Before wading through reams of collateral reading, do some listening. What you already know about the subject will come to mind. You find correlative material everywhere—in the happenings of the day, the newspaper, the magazines you pick up, in conversations—invariably more than you can use.

One method of assembling material is to list topics as they occur to you, regardless of order. Keep a pad and pencil handy at all times, even by your bed, so that you may jot them down as they come to thought. These points soon begin to fall into a few large groups. Arrange these headings. Although you put them in a certain order, do not be bound by it, for when you give the talk, if your thought is undistracted, the subject matter may unfold in a way superior to your outline.

It is much easier to extemporize than it is to commit to memory. You may have the outline with you when you speak, and do not hesitate to look at it openly if you feel so inclined; listeners will enjoy the pause. Peeking at notes surreptitiously is unnecessary. It has been my experience that it is not helpful to write out what I want to say. I find myself groping for the clever words I used when I wrote instead of seeing the idea they stand for. A word or phrase to remind me of the idea and a thorough understanding of the subject leaves me much freer in my talks than trying to recall what I wrote down. There is a chapter "To Commit to Memory" on page 217 in case this is required of you. Otherwise extemporize.

Even in a formal lecture, talk informally. Informal diction

is our natural way of giving ideas. The formality may be in your subject or in the nature of the gathering, but do not let it be in your presentation. If your formost desire is to convey ideas, your manner of speaking should be conversational.

From the outset, have interest in the audience. Enjoy them. *Think of them, not of what they may be thinking of you.* Enjoy the introducer, if you have one. You may even exchange a friendly remark with him while waiting to begin, rather than sitting stiffly gazing at the audience. Listen, listen, listen! It keeps your thought turned away from yourself; it gives you inspiration. Listen to the introduction. It is a part of a complete whole. You can let it start you on your speech. When you are filled with your subject, you can lead up to it from any angle.

If you are a man and your introducer is a woman, you will rise as she rises to begin the introduction. Then sit down until she comes to the formal presentation, when you again rise. It used to be customary to rise when your name was first mentioned, but this convention has been more or less abandoned because so many introducers mention the name early in the talk. If you rise then, the attention of the audience turns to you and does not follow the introduction. Your interest is in a clear presentation of a subject and the introduction is part of it.

After the introduction is concluded, acknowledge it graciously in the manner which is most natural to you. Avoid falling into the worn-out words and phrases heard so often that they have lost their meaning. A simple "Thank you," sincerely spoken, is better than borrowed speeches. Take time to look at the introducer as you say it. The audience will not run away. When you turn back to them, feel that you are with them, drawn together by a common interest—the ideas contained in your talk.

Listen alertly as you stand there. Fear would cause you to hurry. Love of your subject and of your audience gives you poise enough to wait until you have perfect silence. Coughing, clearing of throats, rustling of paper, shifting in seats, stops quickly with the quiet listening of the speaker, but will continue for several minutes if the talk starts before the disturbance is stilled. If you place a high value on what you are saying, you will refuse to talk above any confusion. Waiting impatiently for the audience to be still will not quiet them. Impatience stirs them up; calmness quickly gains their attention.

Do not hesitate to set aside any object that has been placed between you and your listeners. People love informality and ease in a speaker. For more details on this turn to the chapter "On the Platform," page oo.

Instead of warming up to your subject, start visualizing immediately. Have a good attack on the first words you speak. Do not run down at the end of sentences. This is more likely to occur when a speech has been memorized than when extemporizing, but some have this tendency at any time. Thoughtfully finish each idea.

You will often be as interested as the audience in the way a talk shapes itself when you let inspiration direct. A poet in an unrehearsed book discussion over the radio, after making a particularly brilliant remark, showed unconcealed pleasure in it, as if it had been given by someone else and came as a complete surprise to him. You can often have this same experience if you extemporize.

The faces of the audience can help to guide you as to how long to remain on a certain topic. This is one of the beauties of not being entirely bound by an outline, or, worse yet, by memorized words. However, when you see people enjoying one particular angle do not become intoxicated with your success and continue with it even after inspiration says, "Move on." You will not do this if you keep your listening ear ever on guard. On the other hand, do not hurry over some particular phase of the subject before you have sufficiently developed it. Be with the point you are making. The one to come will take care of itself when you reach it.

Pauses are almost as important as the words themselves. Seldom are there enough or adequate pauses in a speech. Space sets off the object it surrounds. The pause after an idea shows the value you place upon it. A profound idea needs a substantial pause to let the listener grasp its full significance. You yourself will unconsciously make such a pause if you are thinking of what you say. You can keep people thinking with you on an idea until you take a fresh breath to start the next sentence. Experiment. Make a statement and stay with it, ponder it for some moments before taking a breath. Notice how its value unfolds to you, and you will feel the same thing happening to your audience. Of course pauses that are overlong break the continuity of your talk. Listen for the right length pause for each thought you present.

It is a mistake to talk too long. An audience can become surfeited if it is given too much at one time. Alertness on your part will tell you as clearly as a stop-and-go signal how much your audience is ready to take. Heed the audience reaction. Keep within the allotted time. It is better to leave out certain points and to present a few points clearly than to touch upon many superficially and leave the audience confused.

Committing a speech to memory is the cause of many uninteresting lectures, although it is possible for memorized words to be as convincing as extemporized ones. This incident illustrates what may happen: A man gave a lecture on a rainy night. The audience was small, the hall large and barnlike—a depressing experience for any lecturer. The topic sounded as if it should be interesting—the talk contained good material, the words were well pronounced, the emphasis correct for the meaning, the lecturer's posture was easy and his gestures natural. Yet afterwards no one could remember any of the points the speaker had made. The only part which could be clearly recalled was his final, hearty, "Good evening, my friends." Why was this? Because he had committed his speech to memory, and, owing to his disappointment at the poor attendance, he allowed himself to speak with no thought behind his words. Had he been extemporizing, he could not have indulged his mood, but would have had to put his mind on what he was doing. Better to mispronounce words, hesitate, even use poor construction, than have faultless delivery with no motivation of thought to give it life. Fine-sounding speeches without accompanying thought have no substance. *Sincerity, that is, thinking of what you say as you say it, is a "must" in speaking.*

If the choice rests with you whether you should write your speech and read it or extemporize, choose the latter. An eminent mathematician and physicist was invited to speak at a college near his laboratory. The men were delighted with his talk and asked him back in a short time. When he came again, instead of speaking he read his material. This time they were frankly bored. He did not know how to make ideas live when reading. The few ideas he gave in speaking were more useful than the many he covered in his prepared paper.

After a speech is made you still have an obligation toward it. You need to support it and keep it impersonal. Pride often causes a speaker to apologize when told how much one enjoyed his talk. This accentuates the few rough places in the performance which would otherwise go unnoticed. Never personalize and limit your talks. Continually give the ideas prime importance in your thought, and they will also be of prime importance in the thought of your hearers.

TO COMMIT TO MEMORY

TO COMMIT TO MEMORY

It is necessary, on occasion, to commit words to memory. Some lecturers are required to give their talks verbatim. A few salesmen are forced to use "canned talks"—many insurance companies insisting on them because they are afraid that their men may give inadequate or incorrect explanations of their policies. Often political speeches must be read or committed to memory in order to present the exact policy of a party and also in order to publish the speech substantially as it was given. All actors are expected to stay with the words of the play.

However, I would advise extemporizing unless the occasion absolutely demands a memorized speech. Contrary to general opinion, it is much more difficult to speak well when repeating memorized words than it is when extemporizing. The mistaken belief that the clear saying of the words will put over their meaning has caused many uninteresting and ineffectual talks. When you speak from memory it is too easy to say words without thinking of their meaning. As I have said before, the thinking is to your speaking what paint is to the artist. Without it you can form no pictures.

To commit a talk to memory, first know how to read it conversationally. No mere learning of the words with the expectation that later you will give them with their right interpretation. I have had people come to me for help with a lecture who had already learned it with unnatural emphasis and could never drop the wrong pattern. Unless you can read as naturally as you speak, you are almost certain to commit words to memory with the same incorrect emphasis with which you read them. Study and practice the reading instructions given in Part II of this book.

Otis Skinner's wife, Maud Durbin, wrote of studying a part with Madam Modjeska: "Over and over we read our parts together. . . . She did not memorize her lines—she absorbed the character. . . . My immature method had been to commit the lines at once to memory. This was a heinous fault, and she scolded me roundly."

Using the same technique, you should read your lines until you absorb the ideas they stand for and the words you read sound as if they were being spoken for the first time, not merely repeated. Read them until the emphasis, inflection, pauses are exactly like your speaking, until the words vanish and you are conscious only of the idea.

Enrich your understanding of the words which are used. Synonyms and antonyms will often bring them to life better than a complete definition.

Now, after you have the full significance of the script, and can read it conversationally, you are ready to commit it to memory. You will probably find that your thorough understanding of it has already established the words in your thought. "An idea includes all that is necessary for its expression."

Your first reading usually entails a certain amount of editing —even on material prepared for you by another, as sentences which are perfectly logical on paper, often sound stilted and unconvincing when spoken. For a lecture to sound conversational, it must be written in a colloquial way. When working on radio programs publicizing this work, I started by writing the script and then trying to adjust my speaking to what I had written. I soon found that this was not the best way for me to work. I had much better results when I would jot down notes of what I wanted to present and, using these as a springboard, would talk over a tape recorder. I would then write the script from the recording and, of course, it would be written in my natural style of speaking.

After you are satisfied that the written text reads conversationally, ask yourself questions which the words of your script answer. The reason for this interrogation is that when you answer a question, you will most likely use a conversational rhythm and you will also bring out the real meat of your script.

For the sake of experiment, read the following paragraph from one of my scripts. If you have a recorder, record your first reading.

> Think of all the valuable information that is contained in descriptive and instructive pamphlets put out by organizations! Their purpose is to help their employees understand the concern for which they work and the importance of their own position to that concern. Yet how little of it ever reaches their mentalities. If the supervisors of the company could learn to read these pamphlets aloud in a way that would make the workers understand them, or if the supervisors could explain what the pamphlets contain, it would be a real asset to the companies in actual dollars and cents. The better understanding which the employees would gain of their business and the self-respect which would follow a realization of their individual part in the business, would bring an immediate change in their attitude towards their work and also in the human relations of the organization.

Now ask yourself such questions as:

What are we asked to think about?	—the valuable information contained in descriptive and instructive pamphlets
Where do they come from?	—put out by organizations
For what purpose?	—to help their employees understand the concern for which they work

What else?	—the importance of their own position to that concern
What are we asked to think about these pamphlets?	—how little of it ever reaches the workers' mentalities
What would make them more effective?	—if the supervisors of the company could learn to read the pamphlets aloud in a way that would make the workers understand them
Or what alternative?	—or if the supervisors could explain what the pamphlets contain
What would be the result?	—it would be a real asset to the companies in actual dollars and cents
Why?	—the better understanding which the employees would gain of their business and the self-respect which would follow a realization of their individual part in the business
Would do what?	—would bring an immediate change in the human relations of the organization

After reading the answers, look away from the script and give the words exactly as you would say them. If they sound different from the way you have been reading them, mark the change in some way so that you will not lose the conversational pattern.

> For example, in the last answer you might find you had emphasized *immediate* instead of the key words: *bring, change, human relations.* You can find the vital words in a passage if you will think of how you would send the thought it contains to someone in a telegram.

Don't neglect the pauses—especially if your subject is profound. Mark them. They are almost as important as the text.

Without the pauses the words cannot expand into their full meaning. Lack of pause is one of the worst faults in verbatim talks.

Never practice the words of the speech without thinking of the meaning. Always move out from the seeing of the idea, not from the remembering of words.

Even when the talk is verbatim you can give examples or stories extemporaneously. They usually will brighten your presentation and get you back into a conversational rhythm, in case you have slipped into a "learned-by-heart" tone.

If you have an introducer listen to what he has to say. You can sometimes comment on it, which is always gratifying to him or even tie the introduction into your lecture by a few opening remarks before taking up the lecture proper.

Forgetting your speech is often caused by reaching ahead for what you should say next. One speaker who had this difficulty found that as he thought only of the meaning of the words of the moment, he was ready for what came next and could remember his talk, whereas reaching ahead for the next sequence diverted his attention from what he was saying and made him lose the natural continuity of the talk.

To summarize: Be sure that your text is written in a conversational style. Before you try to commit to memory, learn to read it so that it sounds as spontaneous as your speaking. Never practice the words thoughtlessly. Allow substantial thinking pauses where they are needed. Ask yourself questions (as shown in the example given), which can be answered by the words of your speech. This will keep your reading of the talk alive, cause you to vary the tempo, and force you to arrive somewhere at the end. Then, if you keep your eye on the ball, listen to the meaning of the word at the moment you say it, your talk will be newly born each time, and even though the lecture is given verbatim it will sound natural and be convincing.

FREE EXPRESSION

FREE EXPRESSION

Free expression, wherever and in whatever form it may appear, is an experience. For instance, Raymond Massey's reading in the production of *John Brown's Body*—nothing between the audience and the character he portrayed. Again that selflessness and rapt devotion to the idea came to light in a Horowitz concert, taking form in an accuracy of technique, a rhythm of body, a magnificence of performance, that made the listeners want to rise to their feet and shout for the sheer joy of being on hand when it happened. It was like having seen a shooting star stream across the sky, or a rainbow so close that you could see where it ended on the green hillside, drenching it with liquid color. Free expression is an experience!

And its basic laws are those used in this study of reading and speaking: Listening, that eliminates all self-consciousness and opens wide to idea-consciousness; an alive valuing of the idea, putting it before all else; an obedient expression of it, inspired enough to overcome every limitation which might dim its purity.

These laws can be utilized in any artistic expression, but they apply as well to the way you play games, or conduct your business. The truth is that these laws apply to all conscious activities.

In a class in Freedom in Expression, the assignment was consciously to value ideas during the coming week. A sculptor taking the course realized that he had never valued himself or his art sufficiently. He turned to some of his sketches which he had laid aside and found one which had real merit. Valuing the idea back of the sketch led him to model a magnificent statue of David, excellent enough to be used at the entrance of one of the principal buildings of a world's fair.

A sportsman discovered that learning to listen, to focus on each word he read, helped him to keep his eye on the ball in golf, and improved his game.

In another case a woman whose opportunities had been limited, was so conscious of this limitation that she was awkward and unsure of herself when around people and was seldom invited to social functions. Through gaining a true sense of poise, she found doors opened to her that had formerly been closed.

Have you been using your talents to the fullest? Do you frequently have the satisfaction of free expression? If not, the chart inside the cover of this book may help you. It illustrates the causes of frustration—why some ideas are suppressed or poorly presented. It also shows that when an idea is freely expressed you have genius.

Do not place the thought of genius far away from yourself up on some pedestal. *Genius is only you, freed from self, clear-sighted, and unafraid.*

*Description of Chart**

In this chart the idea is pictured as light, enlightenment; the smaller circles represent individuals who are exposed to the idea. The expression of the idea is shown by the reflected light coming out from the individual thought, seen in diagrams numbers 3, 4, 5, 6.

No. 1 represents the introvert thought which is not even conscious of the idea, although exposed to it. This thought does not listen; it is completely self-centered.

No. 2 shows a thought which sees the idea but is separated from it by a negative viewpoint which promptly stifles any urge toward expression. "To be negatively electrified is to repel all good."

* See end papers.

No. 3 show the way most of us express ideas. This thought is aware of the idea and is expressing it, but in a mediocre way. Here are some of the causes of this limitation:

　a. Concern about what someone thinks of you. This includes either a desire for praise or a fear of criticism. In both cases you are noting where the idea is going, not looking at the idea—like looking at where you are going to put the ball, instead of keeping your eye on the ball. If you are wholly with the idea you cannot be worried about how it will be received.

　b. A sense of responsibility about what you do, which causes anxiety and tenseness. This person's attitude is, "I have to say something, and I'll go through with it if it kills me," instead of, "I have something to say."

　c. Conventionality, apathy, indifference. These cause imitation, a lack of freshness and originality, either from fear of being different, or from not being sufficiently interested in the idea to stay with it.

No. 4 is not separated from the idea by any barrier except distance. This thought has an alert interest and has good expression, but is still conscious of technique. The majority of our public performers belong here. When we see such a performer, we talk of his great range of voice, the speed of his fingers, his clear enunciation. Many remain at this level of development, either because they are not alert enough, or humble enough to turn wholly to the idea for direction—satisfied to remain with self-conscious expression.

No. 5 is the same as No. 4 except that this thought is drawing closer to the idea and the expression is becoming more impersonal and higher in quality.

No. 6 represents free expression. Here self is completely submerged in the seeing and being of the idea. You look at or listen to this person and are aware of the idea alone. He is master of his technique and does not give conscious thought to it, nor to what anyone thinks, nor to himself. Every part of him moves in perfect obedience to the idea. When this state is reached you have GENIUS. This one not only sees the idea, but embodies it; he seems to be the very presence of it.

The difference between genius and talent is pointedly made in the following quotations:

> Talent is that which is in a man's power;
> Genius is that in whose power a man is.
>
> —JAMES RUSSELL LOWELL

> Genius does what it must;
> Talent does what it can.
>
> —BULWER LYTTON

"Genius is perfection of technique plus something else," Hendrik van Loon wrote. He explained that he did not know exactly what this "something else" was, but that he knew it any time he saw it. Later he implied that it might be inspiration.

Should *technique* be placed before *inspiration* in defining genius? Technique alone never made a genius.

One young woman, after five years of college training in speech, found that well-pronounced words, breath control, all the technical points she had learned, failed her when she wanted to speak. She complained about it to one of her professors, who told her that the school could only give her the technique, but that a mental something must take place before she could master the art.

Unfortunately educators often are unable to do more for their students than give them techniques which have been successfully used by competent persons. This is not enough. To fill the need for a right mental approach, this book has focused constantly on *listening* and *valuing*. Without these, the technique is powerless to bring free expression.

BUT technique has an important place; the many time-proved methods are useful tools, but the inspiration of ideas needs to be *first*. It will motivate the study. The one who discovers and visualizes an idea and studies technique in order that he may express it accurately, learns more quickly and works harder than the one who studies technique as an end in itself. And he does not stop with what he learns, but he will invent new techniques the better to meet his demands on himself for an exact statement of the idea. "An idea includes all that is necessary for its expression."

Think of the way the Wright brothers built their first airplane. They couldn't follow the technique of anyone else. They had to invent their own, helped of course by the failures of other inventors. But they saw an idea so clearly that they were able to do just this—invent their own technique. They did not stop with the first crude expression. The idea attracted to itself many useful inventions and techniques which would perfect and speed up production.

As education shows us how to listen, we shall start with the "something else" of which Van Loon spoke, the inspiration which brings originality and success to an invention, an art, or a science.

Katherine Mansfield, famous New Zealand short story writer, strove for that "something else" in her work, writing in her journal: "Lord, make me crystal clear for thy light to shine through. . . . I wonder why it should be so difficult to be humble . . .

"Calm yourself, clear yourself. One must learn, one must practice to *forget* oneself. I can't tell the truth about Aunt Anne unless I am free to enter into her life without self-consciousness. I must try to write simply, fully, freely, from my heart. Quietly, caring nothing for success or failure, but going on. . . ."

Toscanini's capacity to lose self and "be the idea" in a musical score illustrates what the interpreter must do in reading as well as in music. With purity of heart and consecration to the music, he seemed to wipe out of his thought all previous renditions of a masterpiece, and to get back to the idea which caused the composing of the score. This idea should determine the interpretation as well. Toscanini worked tirelessly until his musicians also saw the idea, because he knew that, if they could but see this idea, its motivating power would direct their playing of every note. One senses, as he listens to music directed by such a genius as Toscanini, that it is not merely a rehearsal of retold strains that he hears, but that he is face to face with the thing itself. Toscanini was so humble that, when his orchestra burst into applause at a rehearsal, because they realized the heights to which he had lifted them, he said with tears in his eyes, "It is not me. It is Beethoven." Yet this humility was before the idea only, not before persons. A stern master, with no patience for slovenliness, he worked his men relentlessly, demanding perfection, refusing to allow anything to dim the purity of the rendering. His unselfed dedication to an idea shows in the fact that he postponed for years the recording of Beethoven's Ninth Symphony until he felt that he had fully realized the idea back of the music.

You can learn from Toscanini how to be a better reader or speaker. Notice step by step the qualities he had—purity of heart, consecration to the idea, the wiping out of previous renditions (no imitation), working tirelessly to see the idea, humility, selflessness, no patience with slovenliness, demand for perfection of statement—an arresting array.

All real artists use the idea as the starting point and work out from it. You feel its rhythm throughout whatever they do. Unafraid to depart from the conventional, they give with spontaneity and originality, dedicating themselves to clear visualization. Such as these offer an order based on law, and law is for all men.

All have the qualities of greatness. That which made Benjamin Franklin and Leonardo da Vinci different from the rest is that they found free expression for the ideas which came to them. Ideas come to everyone. How few give them free rein!

But if you understand the laws which great people have used, you yourself can be freed from many limitations. Why do you live synthetically when you have the capacity for real experience? Why are you satisfied merely to read news, adventure, travel stories, and see motion pictures when you should be making current events yourself? Ideas should push you out into broader fields, perhaps writing a book, helping your community, or even opening up a dormant country.

You need not wait for some idea which will set the world afire before you start, but try to apply the laws of free expression every day. Listen for ideas; value them, stay with them; express them with relish and spontaneity, and free expression will be yours.

KEY TO TRANSCRIPTIONS
USED IN THIS BOOK

KEY TO TRANSCRIPTIONS
USED IN THIS BOOK

Any effort to show what the voice does in reading or speaking is necessarily artificial, because as soon as we listen to the voice, that which gives it the natural emphasis, pitch, inflection, intensity—the thinking—is divided. Even at the risk of making you self-conscious for a time, it is necessary to correct mistakes common to reading aloud. Otherwise you continue to make them, totally unconscious that you are not reading the way you speak. At a glance these corrections may look complicated, but taken slowly and tried out thoughtfully as you go along, they are not difficult.

Follow the transcriptions first. See where it differs from the way you usually read. Then try to read from the actual text and let the thought be foremost instead of the pattern.

A word underlined (as Lord) should be valued—always through the vowel sound. Watch not to hit such words from the outside, but rather to think through them.

s	under a word means see it, say it slowly, stretch it.
S	before a phrase means read it more slowly than the previous text.
F	before a phrase means read it faster.
	A line under a beginning vowel means a slight attack on it. "He came in." Not "He cae min."
( )	around syllables, words, or phrases, means to slight them, sometimes by reading them more rapidly, sometimes at a lower level, always without

emphasis, because they add no new idea to the picture.

A line under a whole phrase means to hold it together: "If I make my bed in hell." A figure of speech. We do not want to visualize someone making a bed.

H or **||**   over a word means read at a higher level.

. . .   means pause, varying according to the number of dots used.

∧   means pause also.

_____   is to show comparative pitch and tempo, the word under the symbol corresponding to the symbol's time and pitch.

You don't?

    O   shows an accented syllable.

    −   shows an unaccented syllable.

    Ↄ   The curve shows the glide of the voice, the voice following the direction of the curve.

↙   Indicates the application of the law just stated.

The curve under a word also shows the glide of the voice. Thus:

"no"   means a positive downward emphasis.

"no"   a questioning, as if you implied, "You don't think so?"

"not me"   the voice follows the bend of the line in a circumflex.

L   come in on lower level.

H   come in on higher level.

1, 2, 3 etc. under words or phrases indicates a building up. When you see these you will unconsciously come in on different levels.

[ ]   Explanation, not to be read aloud.

ch   Change of mood.

com   A command. Read as such.

nar   Read as simple narrative.

med   Read meditatively.

A tie bar between two phrases means make very little pause: "The man, as he journeyed. ..."

The Bible transcriptions are written without break between the verses in order to preserve their continuity.

Italicized words in the Bible are words added by the translator —not in the original, and are usually unstressed.

Index

Accent; *see also* Emphasis
  in comparisons, 84
  incorrect, on prepositions, 75-76
Accented syllables, 64, 65, 72, 73, 89;
  see also Unaccented syllables
Acting, 24, 25, 37, 47-49, 60, 95, 96, 115,
  122, 125, 154, 165, 167, 217, 218
Agassiz, Louis, 176
Ah, O, 131-32
American Dictionary, 76
Announcements, 32, 33, 206-208
Antonyms, 27-28, 33, 34-35, 41, 44-45,
  101, 103, 119, 148-49, 150, 218
Apologizing, 23, 25, 28, 127, 149, 178-
  79, 204
Art, 48, 49-50
Art Spirit, The (Henri), 17
Articles *(the, a),* 63
Assembling material, 209
Attention, how to hold, 42, 53, 68, 179,
  191, 207, 211
Audience
  reaction of, 211, 212
  unity with, 104, 161, 166, 168-69, 210
  visualizing of, 104, 166, 207

Barrymore, Ethel, 60
Beecher, Henry Ward, 108
Beethoven, Ludwig van, 10-11, 230
Beethoven—The Man and the Artist
  . . . (Kerst and Krehbiel), 11
Bernhardt, Sarah, 24
Bible references
  Gen. 3:6, 139
    32:24-30, 132-33
  Exod. 3:13, 75
    4:2-4, 75
  I Kings 3:11, 143-44
  I Chron. 29:11, 131

Ps. 16:8, 9, 85
  23, 55-58, 83, 122
  33:6-9, 136
  34:17, 19, 141
  40:1-2, 34-35
  46:2-3, 117, 118
  93, 126
  94:1, 86
  111:1-4, 6, 7, 77-78
  139:7-10, 91
  145:15, 75
Prov. 28:13, 83
Eccles. 1:2, 141
  2:4-5, 121, 122
Isa. 14:16-17, 82
  33:10, 22, 139
  40:11, 140
  40:28, 81-82
  44:6, 87
  45:5-6, 134
  45:9-13, 138
  54:10, 76
  54:17, 135-36
  55:8-9, 142
Dan. 3:4-6, 128
Matt. 5:13-16, 28-29
  7:7-11, 133
  7:17-20, 136
  7:24-27, 139-40
  11:28, 76
  14:30, 86
  25, 25-26
Mark 12:30, 139
Luke 2:16, 69
  4:36-37, 128
  10:31-34, 119-21
  12:13-15, 69
John 4:9-11, 24, 127
  5:5-9, 71

John 8:44, 125
    8:57-58, 75
    9:1-4, 135
    13:34, 35, 79
    13:36, 86
    17:5, 86
Rom. 8:1-2, 134-35
    8:6, 84
    8:24-25, 85
    8:38-39, 89-90
    12:21, 80
I Cor. 1:26-29, 137
    13:1, 85
    13:4, 78
    13:7, 91-92
    13:9-11, 73-74
    14:17, 116
    15:53-54, 137
II Cor. 4:15, 141
    4:18, 83
    6:16, 133
Eph. 3:20-21, 73
Phil. 4:8, 142-43
Col. 1:16, 76
    2:8, 135
I. Thess. 5:15, 141
Jas. 1:2-3, 141
    1:6, 69
I John 3:1-3, 129-30
    3:3, 142
Jude 24-25, 140
Rev. 21:3, 68
Bragging, 179, 192
Breathing, 68, 94, 95-98, 100, 101
Browning, Robert, 173
Business meetings, 182-88

Carver, Dr. George Washington, 18
Cerf, Bennett, 195
Church services, 167
Churchill, Sir Winston, 79, 105, 180
Circumflex; *see* Inflection
Clichés, 177, 178, 205, 210
Climax, building up to, 90-91, 130-31, 138-39
"Comparisons are odorous," 26, 202

Comparisons, to read, 84-85
Concept, 10
Conferences, 183-88
Confidence, self, 22-30, 165, 174
Consonant sounds, 63-64, 105-106, 111-13
Continuity, 181
    in reading, 76-80, 136-38
Contrasts, 135, 139-40, 142
    law of, 84
    of negatives, 58, 83
    of prepositions, 76
Conversation, 189-96
    defined, 189
    difference between reading and, 53-54
    impersonal, 190
    unity in, 195
Conversational pronunciation, 63-66, 118
Conversational style, 61-62, 65, 105, 210
    in memorized speeches, 218-20, 221
    in reading, 42, 67-93, 117, 135, 142-44
Copeland, Charles Townsend, 195
Crabb's English Synonyms, 189
Crosby, Bing, 38

Daydreaming, 18-19
Descartes, 9
Diction, 105-14; *see also* Pronunciation
    correction of, 53-54, 61-66
Direct address, 85-87
Direct discourse, 115, 126-28
    pause before, 69
Drummond, Henry, 30
Dunn, Emma, 5
Durbin, Maud, 218
Duse, Eleanora, 24

Editing a speech, 218-19
Education, listening the key to, 19-20, 229
    aim in, 5
Egotism, 22, 23, 36, 102, 178
Emerson, Ralph Waldo, 43
Empathy, 50, 125
Emphasis, 35, 57, 73, 77, 78, 79, 116, 130, 163, 217, 218

false, 35, 57, 73, 77, 79, 116, 130, 163, 217

English language, 105-14

Entering a room, 159

Exhaustive Concordance of the Bible; see Strong's *Bible Dictionary*

Expectancy, 13, 16, 46, 148, 173, 174, 183, 198, 200

Expression
  contained within idea, 9, 10, 15, 161, 218, 229
  defined, 9
  free, 5-6, 225-31
  inspiration and, 12
  science of, 5-6
  three steps of, 12-15, 31, 197-98, 225

Extemporaneous speaking, 173-79, 201, 205, 207, 209, 211, 213, 217, 221

Eye contact, 167, 168

Failure, fear of, 41

Formal occasions, 61-62, 161-62, 209-10

Franklin, Benjamin, 29, 230

Freedom
  of expression, 5-6, 225-31
  from mannerisms, 160
  of thought, 17
  of voice, 94-104

Funk and Wagnalls Dictionary, 189

Genius, 13, 50, 151, 226, 228, 230
  definition of, 226
  description of chart of, 226-28

Gesture, 49, 167

"Gettysburg Address," 12

Gide, 122-23

Graciousness, 29, 101, 150-51, 165, 210

Guide-Posts to Chinese Painting (Hackney), 67

Habits; *see also* Mannerisms
  speech, 102, 106, 176-77
  spontaneity and, 40
  strength of, 43
  visualizing retarded by, 36

Hackney, Louise M., 68

Hands, 158, 164, 165

Hegel, 9

Henri, Robert, 17, 30, 35, 43

Hesitation, 23, 151, 176

Highlights in reading, 57, 117-18

Horowitz, Vladimir, 50, 225

Ideas
  characteristics of, 9-10
  defined, 9
  discovery of, through listening, 18, 173-74
  expression included within, 9, 10, 15, 38, 148, 161, 218, 229
  identification with, 37, 45, 47, 50
  impersonality of, 9, 10, 28, 161, 179
  rhythm of, 47, 50

Identification
  with ideas, 37, 47, 227-28
  with words, 129-32

Imagination, 19, 31

Imitation, 32, 39, 43, 49, 112, 177, 182, 200

Impersonality
  in conversation, 190
  in direct address, 86
  of ideas, 9, 10, 28, 161, 179
  in reading, 115-16, 122-23, 125, 126
  in selling, 197

Inadequacy, sense of, 23, 27

Inferiority and superiority, 22, 150, 151, 198

Inflection; *see also* Voice
  determined by meaning, 76
  in direct address, 86
  in questions, 80-82
  rising, 57, 74, 89-90, 202-3
  in series, 89-90

Informality
  in conferences, 184
  in the formal lecture, 209-10
  on the platform, 162, 168, 211

Inspiration, 12, 13, 15, 21, 48, 49, 100, 228-29; *see also* Listening
  in reading, 116, 119, 132
  in speaking, 173, 174, 177, 180, 182, 198, 200, 202, 211

Intellectuality, 17, 31, 194

International Phonetic Association, 108

Interruption, 169-70, 186, 192-94
Introductions, 164, 168, 204-6, 210
Intuition, 18, 21, 47, 148
Iturbi, José, 103

Jesus, 28
    parables of, 25-26, 119-21
John Brown's Body, 225
Jungle Book (Kipling), 16

Kenyon, John S., 65
Kipling, 16
Kropotkin, Princess Alexandra, 196

Language, English, 105-14
Lanier, Sidney, 87
"Last Supper" (Leonardo), 123
Laughton, Charles, 12
Lazarus, Harry, 196
Lecky, Prescott, 30
Lecturing; *see* Public speaking
Lehmann, Lotte, 32
Leonardo da Vinci, 123, 230
Levels, voice, 79-80, 91-93; *see also* In-
    flection
Limitations, self-made, 174-75
Lincoln, Abraham, 12
Listening
    to diction, 108
    and discrimination, 20, 47, 115, 119
    to ideas, 12-13, 16-21, 23, 31, 49, 50,
        59, 115, 119, 123-24, 126, 130, 147,
        161, 170, 173, 174, 197-98, 199, 209,
        210, 211, 225, 228
    as key to learning, 19-20
    to others, 23, 162, 164-65, 190, 193,
        194, 195-96, 210
    in reading, 115, 123-24, 126, 130
    rhythm and, 49
    self-consciousness and, 13, 20-21, 147,
        161, 225
Locke, 9
Losing last words by dropping the
    voice
    in reading, 79-80, 137, 139
    in speaking, 176, 191, 211
"Lost Ten Tribes, The" (Wild), 114
Lowell, Amy, 24

Lowell, James Russell, 180-81, 228
Lytton, Bulwer, 28, 228

Mannerisms, 162-63, 176
Mansfield, Katherine, 229
Masefield, John, 72
Massey, Raymond, 225
Master of ceremonies, 23, 205
Maynor, Dorothy, 147
Meetings
    conducting of, 182-88
    speaking in, 180-81
Memorized speeches, 201, 205, 212, 217-
    21
Merman, Ethel, 25
Millay, Edna St. Vincent, 86
Modesty, false, 22, 23
Modjeska, 218
Monosyllables, unstressed, 65-66, 77
Mood, showing it in reading, 32, 85-86,
    115, 126-28
    reading against emotional, 122-24,
    137
Mortimer, Raymond, 196

Nasal tone, 98-99, 110
Naturalness, 1, 2, 26, 38, 42, 53, 62, 63,
    101, 151, 153, 160, 162, 170, 178,
    201, 210, 219
Nazimova, 49, 125
Negatives, to read, 58, 83, 135
Negative thinking, 23, 24, 41, 94, 95,
    173-74, 185, 198, 226
New-idea words, 15, 47, 73, 76, 77, 78,
    91, 137
Niten, Myamoto, 50
Notes, use of, 166, 184, 209

Observation, improving diction
    through, 113
Originality, 6, 15, 36, 43, 229, 230

Party People (Lazarus), 196
Pauses, 67-72, 88, 118, 126, 128, 148,
    173, 176, 212, 220-21
    in conversation, 190
    on entering a room, 159
    in meetings, 185

People, The (Sandburg), 93
Personal pronouns, 132-33
Perspective in reading, 117-21
Phelps, William Lyon, 60
Phrasing, 69, 76
Platform work, 160-70, 209-13
Plato, 9, 37
Poise, 29, 147-52, 153, 156, 159, 161, 198
   synonyms and antonyms for, 148-49, 150
Pope, Alexander, 108
Positiveness, 27, 148, 173, 174, 176
Posture, 153-59, 164, 165
Praise, its dangers, 28
Prepositions, 75-76
Pronunciation, 106, 107, 108-13; *see also* Diction
   conversational, 63-66, 118
Public speaking, 160-70, 209-13
Punctuation, 69, 76
Pure reading; *see* Reading, impersonality in
Purpose, 16, 103
   define, 170, 184
   keeping to, in meetings, 182, 183
   unity of, 164, 199

Questions, 80-82
   stimulate thinking, 32, 56, 57, 184, 187, 219-21
   stimulate conversation, 185, 191, 192
Quietness, 12, 50, 199

Reading aloud, 4-5, 115-44
   carelessness in, 140-41
   consciousness of mood in, 86, 115, 126-8
   conversational style in, 42, 63, 67-93, 117-18, 135, 142-44
   fine art of, 115-44
   identifying with words in, 129
   impersonality in, 115-23, 125, 126
   laws of, 67-93
   listening and, 115, 123-24, 126, 130
   mental approach to, 122-25, 129, 130, 167-68
   need for, 4, 53
   oneness with listeners in, 161, 168

   pitfalls in, 53-54
   as preparation for effective speaking, 53-60
   rhythm and tempo in, 46-47, 58, 59-60, 71-72, 87-88, 91, 93, 119, 126-27, 136
   self-disciplining in, 58, 60
   technique in, 116-21
   timing in, 53-60, 67, 117
   turning pages when, 170
   valuing step in, 14-15
   visualizing in, 31, 58, 115, 130, 136
   word meaning and, 54-59
Reasoning, 17, 38
Reasoning words, 85
Recording of voice, 103
Renascence (Millay), 86-87
Repetition
   avoiding monotony in, 142-44
   in improving diction, 113
   slighting in, 77-78, 120, 130, 136, 137
Reports, reading of, 84-85
Rhythm, 44-50
   art and, 49-50, 230
   of environment, 46
   of ideas, 47, 50
   in reading, 46-47, 58, 59-60, 71, 126, 136
   self-will and, 49
   in speaking, 46, 63, 105
   synonyms and antonyms for, 44-45
   technique and, 48-49, 119
   of youth, 46
Rising, 158
Robert's Rules of Order, 182
Rogers, Will, 150, 191
Roget's Thesaurus, 27, 33, 34, 44-45, 56, 103, 174
Rubato, 47; *see also* Tempo
Ruml, Beardsley, 18
Ruskin, 43

Sandburg, Carl, 93
Seating arrangement, 164, 184
Self-appraisal, 202
Self-confidence, 22-30, 147, 160, 174
Self-consciousness, 13, 20-21, 88, 147, 158, 161, 176, 183, 190, 225, 229

Self-consistency, 30
Self-depreciation, 22, 101
Self-discipline, 58, 60, 156
Self-indulgence, 181
Self-will, 49
Selling, 31-32, 197-203
Series, 89-91, 92, 130-31, 142
  build-up in, 142-44
Shakespeare, 26, 60
Sikorski, Igor, 18
Sincerity, 95, 101, 160, 170, 189, 201, 210, 213
Sitting posture, 158
  on the platform, 158, 164
Socrates, 129
Song of the Chattahoochee, The (Lanier), 87
Speaking
  conversational style in, 61-62
  exemporaneous, 173-79, 201, 207, 209, 211, 213, 217, 221
  in meetings, 180-81
  memorized, 201, 205, 212, 217-21
  public, 160-70, 209-13
  rhythm in, 46, 63
  stopping at the right time, 174
  to correct habits of, 79, 105-14, 176, 191
  visualizing in, 36
Spontaneity, 38-43, 48, 177
  habits and, 40
  imitation and, 39
  in reading, 42
  synonyms and antonyms for, 41
Standing posture, 153-54, 156, 159
Strong's Bible Dictionary, 34, 35, 92, 119
Studying, visualizing an aid to, 35
Superiority and inferiority, 150, 151, 166, 195, 198
Superlatives, 89
Synonyms, 27, 34-35, 56, 119, 136, 218
  for various words, 27-28, 33, 44-45, 56, 148-49, 150

Talents, 226-28
Talking, 189; see also Conservation and Speaking

Technique, 32, 48, 104, 162, 227-29
  of pure reading, 116-21
Temperamental tendencies, 36-37, 95, 101-2
Tempo, 58, 71, 87-88, 99-100, 138
Thompson, Dorothy, 105
Thoreau, Henry, 40, 41
Throat
  clearing of, 102
  open, 94-95, 97, 101, 110
Tilden, William, 109
Timing of speech, 53, 54, 67, 88, 117; see also Tempo
Todd, Professor, 22
Tone; see Inflection and Voice
Toscanini, 121, 229-30
Truth, idea synonymous with, 9, 10

Unaccented syllables, 64, 65, 77, 89
Unexpected happenings, 169-70
Unity
  with audience, 104, 161, 164, 166, 168
  in conversation, 195
  of purpose, 164, 199
Unnaturalness, 42, 62, 148, 160-61, 168, 206

Valuing
  examples of right, 24-26, 28, 29, 225, 226
  of each word, 59
  of ideas, 13-15, 22-25, 31, 68, 70, 101, 190, 225, 228
  of one's ability, 22-30, 101, 161, 202
  of product when selling, 197-98, 202
  synonyms and antonyms for, 27-28
van Loon, Hendrik, 228
Visualizing, 19, 31-37, 72, 77, 84, 90, 91, 93, 105, 117, 119, 124, 128, 149, 155, 182
  of audience, 104, 166, 207
  pauses and, 69, 70-71
  of product when selling, 31, 198
  in reading, 31, 34-35, 58, 130, 135, 136, 139
  retarded by certain habits of thinking, 36
  in speaking, 31, 36, 207

in studying, 35
synonyms and antonyms for, 33
in understanding words, 34-35
Vocabulary increase, 113
Voice; *see also* Inflection
  a focused quality in, 166-67
  freedom of, 94-104, 166
  levels of, 79-80, 91-93
  nasal, 98-99, 110
  recording of, 103
  temperamental tendencies shown in,
    27, 95, 100-102, 125-26
  use of, 94-104
  volume of, 103-4
Volume, 103-4, 124
Vowel sounds, 63, 64, 65, 72-73, 76, 89,
    97-102, 103, 104, 105, 110, 111, 112-
    13

Walking, 154-57, 159

*Webster's New International Diction-
    ary,* 61-62, 65, 76, 112n.
"Were You There When They Cruci-
    fied My Lord?" 147
"West Wind, The" (Masefield) , 72
Whittier, John Greenleaf, 92
Wild, Joseph, 114
Words
  identifying with, 129-30
  increased understanding of, 35, 54,
    119
  new-idea, 15, 47, 54, 59, 73, 76, 77,
    78, 91, 137
  specific, synonyms and antonyms for,
    27-28, 33, 44-45, 56, 148-49, 150
Wright, Frank Lloyd, 43
Wright brothers, 229
Wyld, Professor Henry Cecil, 62

Youth, rhythm of, 46

TALENTED 4.
FINE TECHNIQUE, BUT
LACK OF SELF EFFACEMENT.
GOOD, BUT PERSONAL
EXPRESSION

BRILLIANT 5.
DRAWN CLOSER TO IDEA
ABOUT IS VALUED MORE—
EXPRESSION FREER &
MORE IMPERSONAL.

GENIUS 6.
SELF COMPLETELY
SUBMERGED IN
THE IDEA

IDEA